The Three Tenors

The Three Tenors

Nancy Shear

MetroBooks

MetroBooks

An Imprint of Friedman/Fairfax Publishers

©1998 by Michael Friedman Publishing Group, Inc.

Library of Congress Cataloging-in-Publication data available upon request.

ISBN 1-56799-686-8

Editor: Francine Hornberger
Art Director: Kevin Ullrich
Designer: Meredith Miller
Photography Editor: Wendy Missan
Production Manager: Camille Lee

Color separations by HK Scanner Arts Int'l Ltd.
Printed in China by Leefung-Asco Printers Ltd.

1 3 5 7 9 10 8 6 4 2

For bulk purchases and special sales, please contact:
Friedman/Fairfax Publishers
Attention: Sales Department
15 West 26th Street
New York, NY 10010
212/685-6610   Fax 212/685-1307

Visit our website:
http://www.metrobooks.com

DEDICATION

For my mother, my first and best friend and teacher.

ACKNOWLEDGMENTS

I am deeply grateful to so many people for kindnesses, encouragement, and superb advice.
Among them are:

Barrymore Laurence Scherer, for sharing his great knowledge about the world of singing and singers; Peter G. Davis, Matthew Gurewitsch, and Shirley Fleming, for their important and perceptive suggestions; Carole Adrian and Sara Tornay for their excellent comments; Myron McPherson, a superb vocal coach, for his insights about the voice in general, and the tenor's voice in particular; Dr. Scott M. Kessler, for his illustrations and information on human vocal equipment; Sharon Wagner, for her fine assistance with research; Drs. Phyllis and Eberhard Kronhausen, for their wisdom about the writing of this book, and life in general; Sharyn Rosart, Stephen Slaybaugh, and Francine Hornberger of Michael Friedman Publishing Group, for solid editorial guidance and publishing world advice, all delivered with warmth and encouragement; Betsy Peluso, for her steadfast assistance in reading through the various versions of the manuscript; and author Janice Papolos, whose excellent advice, friendship, and confidence in my ability are forever noted.

Contents

IN 1990, A SINGLE OPERATIC EVENT SO CAPTURED THE IMAGINATION OF THE GENERAL PUBLIC THAT IT BECAME THE GREAT MUSICAL PHENOMENON OF OUR TIME. THREE OPERA SINGERS, JOSÉ CARRERAS, PLÁCIDO DOMINGO, AND LUCIANO PAVAROTTI, JOINED FORCES FOR A CONCERT IN THE ROMAN BATHS OF CARACALLA, HELD JUST BEFORE THE FINAL MATCH OF THE WORLD CUP SOCCER TOURNAMENT.

Above: Placido Domingo (left), Jose Carreras (middle), and Luciano Pavarotti (right) rehearse for the 1990 Three Tenors *concert in Rome.*

The program was seen throughout the world, and the reaction everywhere was the same: enthusiasm that bordered on obsession. Millions of people raced out to get their hands on *Carreras Domingo Pavarotti in Concert* (popularly known as *The Three Tenors*) on CD and video. The response went far beyond anything that could have been predicted: the program, seen by 800 million people, became a best-selling CD, video cassette, and laser disk, reaching numbers more appropriate to rock music; it became the single most powerful fund-raising tool in America's Public Broadcasting System's history; and it has served as an introduction to opera and classical music to people worldwide.

And all this for an art form that, more than any other, is a symbol of elitism. To quickly establish the economic, social, or intellectual high standing of a literary figure or film actor, just put him in a box at the opera. Opera is generally perceived as being prohibitively expensive (one ticket can cost the equivalent of several movie or theater tickets) and very intimidating, requiring formal dress and formal manners, perhaps even a formal education to properly appreciate it. Despite many opera companies trying to make opera more accessible by providing electronic translations at performances, and operas constantly being aired on television, the art form has remained, for the last hundred years or so, primarily in the territory of the elite.

Above: (from left) Three Tenors and one conductor: Plácido Domingo, José Carreras, Zubin Mehta, and Luciano Pavarotti, at the July 16, 1994, concert at Dodger Stadium in Los Angeles. This was their second concert together (the first took place in Rome in 1990), and the first in the United States.

Above: Domingo, Carreras, and Pavarotti, exhibiting a camaraderie that is rare among rivals in the opera world.

To date, more than twelve million CDs, video cassettes, and laser disks of the first Three Tenors concert have been sold. Broadcasts of the Three Tenors concerts have earned enormous amounts of money for the Public Broadcasting System (PBS), which depends on viewers' support for a large percentage of its income. No one knows (or is willing to divulge) the total amount raised by all the Three Tenors programs for all the PBS stations, but an article in the *Washington Post* in March 1991, gave an idea of the type of income the program was generating for these stations. It reported that "those three great tenors singing from the Baths of Caracalla Friday night got Channel 26's spring fundraising drive off to such a fast start the station has now scheduled a fourth performance for the trio's pop concert." The article went on to report that the program had "attracted $120,000 in donations Friday night alone.... A wide-eyed WETA promptly canceled two scheduled Sunday features...." to repeat the *Three Tenors* concert twice, and raised an additional $123,000. "As a result of the unexpected popularity of José, Plácido, and Luciano during the first weekend, the kickoff of WETA's annual spring alms talks earned $286,579 on 5,288 pledges, more than doubling the $126,889 take of the first weekend last year...."

The *Los Angeles Times*, later that month, reported similar dramatic results for other stations: "This was the year," it gushed, "that opera saved public television. Across the nation, public television stations headed into their March pledge drives fearing the worst. Membership was down, donations were slow, and it looked like the only stations that were going to end the drive in the black were the ones that had slashed their goals in anticipation of a slow economy. Just one airing of 'Carreras, Domingo and Pavarotti in Concert with Zubin Mehta' changed everything." A

person taking pledges at WHYY in Philadelphia reported that after the first broadcast of *The Three Tenors* during the fund-raising period, the telephones were "so jammed that they couldn't ring. It was eerie. And it just went on and on." WHYY raised $175,000 during the ninety-minute program, more than had ever been raised by a single program in the station's history. So, the article stated, "they ran it again and again." WHYY ran the program nine times, earning more than $500,000 from it.

KCET in Los Angeles aired it four times, earning more than $600,000, and reached a single-program record of $213,000 for the program's first broadcast. WNET in New York, which aired the program three times in a row on a single day, earned $572,623. WGBH in Boston raised $225,000. Unofficial estimates said the total raised by the program, which was broadcast on ninety public television stations nationwide, was between $4 million and $5 million.

These figures reflect only the initial broadcasts of the first, 1990, Three Tenors program. And although these were the most successful of the Three Tenors broadcasts, subsequent programs continued to bring in substantial funding for PBS, which needed it badly. Not even The Three Tenors themselves predicted their program's success; they opted for a straight fee of $500,000 each rather than take a risk on royalties for what they thought would be limited CD and video sales.

"The Three Tenors" has become a generic term recognizable even to people who have no interest in classical music or opera. Many people who would be hard pressed to identify any other classical musicians are able to recognize the names of the three singers, even if they can't name them on command. In addition to generating interest in opera and revenues from recordings, The Three Tenors have also generated a good deal of controversy.

The phenomenon of a sudden increase in the awareness of opera (or at least of The Three Tenors) has not pleased everyone, especially in the world of classical music. Some music professionals doubt that opera (or symphonic or chamber music) can be properly understood or appreciated by the masses, or if the purely emotional approach to music can be as valid as one that is based on some degree of technical knowledge. They find it hard to believe that the pleasure of a listener who is simply swept along by the beauty of a melody, moved by the poignancy of a phrase, or energized by rhythmic impulses can be as valid as that of someone who gains his or her pleasure by having an awareness of the technical construction of the work, knowing its form, and being able to recognize the most subtle aspects of the performance.

The classical music cognoscenti are most annoyed—some outraged—by what they consider to be distortions of the music, claiming that The Three Tenors exaggerated and cheapened their performances for the sake of wider appreciation. The most severe of the criticisms accused the three of "using" the music for their own advantage, not remaining true to the wishes of the composers by taking liberties that theatricalized the performances and made their own personalities more important than the music itself.

This elitist attitude has not helped to encourage wider appreciation of the art. Some now fear that classical music has a limited life span because so small a percentage of the public cares about it and, therefore, comparatively little money is spent on it.

Classical music retailers hoped that the tremendous interest in the Three Tenors concerts would spread to other classical performers and types of music. Since classical music record sales represent, at best, only about ten percent of total record sales worldwide, almost any increase (even one that would be insignificant in the pop world) would be substantial in the classical world. There has been a ripple effect that has reached general opera and classical music sales, but most of these sales have related in some way only to The Three Tenors, stimulating interest in the complete operas from which their programs' individual arias were taken or of other repertory sung by each of the singers.

The controversy continues: have The Three Tenors helped or hurt classical music? Have the programs served as powerful tools with which to build the diminishing audience for classical music, or have they misrepresented an art form that, in its pure form, would disappoint and bore the newly converted? Were the programs popular because of their strengths, or because of their flaws? Was this really opera at its best, or a cheap form of entertainment? Did the singers compromise themselves and their art to win wide popularity? Can the masses appreciate music in its purest and most subtle form? And most important: why did people respond the way they did?

Since there have been other great opera singers who did not capture the interest of the public on so grand a scale, it is fascinating to consider what this phenomenon is all about, and what its ramifications are for the future. If *The Three Tenors* has generated a new audience for opera, will there be a new generation of great singers available to fill the stages vacated by the now-aging tenors? Will future listeners find music of the past appealing and "relevant"?

In considering all the different aspects of this musical phenomenon, one must heed the lesson of the blind man who tried to describe an elephant by the feel of its different parts. It is important not to lose sight of the one critical element in the case of *The Three Tenors* that is essential to any great performance: the magic generated between the performers themselves, and between the performers and their live and electronic audiences. The Three Tenors drew 800 million viewers into the performance at the Baths of Caracalla in 1990, and 1.3 billion into Dodger Stadium in 1994. Such magic is rare and undefinable but very recognizable. And thank goodness for it.

Below: The Three Tenors' first reunion, at Dodger Stadium in Los Angeles, 1994. Fifty-six thousand people were present, with 1.3 billion people around the world watching on television.

The Tenor and His World

THE OPERA HOUSE
IS A BASTION OF BEAUTY, CREATIVITY, CIVILITY, AND DISCIPLINE. ON A LESS
IMPORTANT LEVEL, IT CAN ALSO BE,
LIKE THE SPORTS ARENA AND THE CIRCUS, A PLACE
WHERE—FROM THE SAFETY AND COMFORT OF ONE'S SEAT—ONE

MAY WITNESS SOMEONE ELSE IN A POSITION OF HIGH DANGER.

THE FACT THAT IT IS NOT A QUESTION OF PHYSICAL DANGER DOES NOT MATTER,

Above: The historic Vienna Staatsoper.
Previous page: The great tenor Lauritz Melchior, playing the Sultan in
a 1955 performance of Arabian Nights, a "musical extravaganza" at the
Jones Beach Marine Theater in Jones Beach, New York. The production also
featured Marily, the elephant, on whose back Melchior made his entrance.

Left: The "old" Metropolitan Opera House, 1883–1966. This beloved house, with plenty of operatic ghosts, was the predecessor of the new building in Lincoln Center.

for when a singer stands on one of the major stages of the world, he is taking risks that can produce major ramifications in his career. At that moment, he is performing for an audience that is as involved and passionate as any audience anywhere.

The tenor range extends basically from C below middle C to the A above middle C, with the possible extension of a few notes in either direction. Not many tenors are able to make beautiful—or even pleasing—sounds above high A, and precious few can extend at all to high D. To sing in the highest regions of the tenor range without sounding forced, with beauty of tone, clear projection, and emotional expressiveness, often while dramatically

sustaining the notes, is a physical feat that is, in the way that the singer uses his body, no less than athletic. It can be a type of high-wire act made more suspenseful by the knowledge that just a tiny bit of phlegm on the vocal cords, or a miscalculated breath, can leave the tenor falling without the equivalent of a safety net. No one (except perhaps members of the rival tenor's claque) wants a tenor to crack his high C, but knowing that it could happen makes the performance all the more exciting. As is said in the opera world, no performance ever recovers from a broken high note.

These high notes are so important that they are referred to as "money notes." They are the ones that most

Above: Australian soprano Dame Joan Sutherland who, with her husband, conductor Richard Bonynge, engaged Pavarotti for a tour of Australia in 1965 that helped to establish his career.

people come to hear, just as dance audiences come to see dancers' leaps. "A truly good tenor is the best box office draw," said the late Kurt Herbert Adler, who was the director of the San Francisco Opera. "There is nothing more exciting than a great high tenor sound."

The ease or difficulty of reaching a high note can be deceptive, as it depends on how one gets there, how such notes are approached. A stepwise approach, with notes leading up to the high pitch, is the least difficult; jumping the gap from a lower pitch to a high one is another story. The nine killer high Cs in the aria "Pour mon âme" in Donizetti's *La Fille du régiment*, for example, are not approached stepwise, by a ladder of notes going right to them, but by a jump up from an octave (the interval of eight steps between two notes of the same name) below.

As important as it may be, the occasional high note—or low note—is not what constitutes the true nature of a part. That is determined by what is called the "tessitura"—the general, or average, range where most of the role lies and where most of the singing is done. Stretching the limits of the voice for a note or two in a single section or aria can cause a bit of strain, but nothing serious; if the tessitura of a given part is too high, however, a singer would be straining for much of the duration of the opera, making a decent performance physically impossible.

A really good tenor, as Schuyler G. Chapin, formerly general manager of the Metropolitan Opera and presently New York City's Commissioner of Cultural Affairs, noted in an article for the October 15, 1973, issue of *The New Yorker*, is the rarest of beasts. "His ringing top notes push the vocal cords to extreme limits. His middle voice must leap the chasm between chest and head registers with

seamless agility. His low tones dip into baritone territory without a hint of growl."

Our preoccupation with the tenor voice is probably due to its being so rare, and to the beauty and overt emotionalism of the roles written for it. Our fascination is also probably due to some primeval appeal. Eric Salzman, in *Stereo Review* magazine in December 1990, offered his analysis of tenor worship: "There is something about the male tenor voice, particularly the Italian version thereof, that evokes images of swooning females, territorial aggression, the gorilla thumping his chest, the alpha male howling down all the other males. This sort of thing is more usually represented nowadays by war heroes, sports stars, film and TV actors, or rock singers. Italian tenoring is not always a subtle expression of the best in human culture, but compared with the alternatives it is certainly a traditional and refined version of male sexuality and aggression."

With notable exceptions, true opera stardom has traditionally been reserved for women. The fiery soprano is the musical parallel of the movie star, with glamour, sex appeal, and temperament in abundance. She—the likes of Geraldine Farrar, Rosa Ponselle, Maria Callas, Renata Tebaldi, Joan Sutherland, and others—inspires almost manic loyalty from fans; rivalries between opera divas are as legendary as some of the performances they sang.

Before The Three Tenors, the tenor who most strongly captured the public's heart was Enrico Caruso (1873–1921), who had become a legend in the truest sense of the word. In addition to exquisite legato (smooth, flowing) phrasing and beauty of tone, Caruso brought tasteful yet heartfelt emotion to operatic singing. As the first great singer to commit his artistry to recordings, Caruso left a legacy that continues to influence singers.

Other great tenors include Giovanni Martinelli (1885–1969), from Italy, known for his superb articulation and remarkable breath control, particularly in the repertory of his native country; Beniamino Gigli (1890–1957), also Italian, highly regarded for the ease and flow of his delivery, which, in lyric and romantic works, made him the natural successor to Caruso, but whose emotionalism (often consisting of excessive sobbing) was not as tastefully expressed as Caruso's; Jussi Björling (1911–1960), a Swede who was beloved for his elegance, beauty of tone, and depth of interpretation, mostly in Italian repertory

(Björling's only weakness was that his voice did not project powerfully); Tito Schipa (1888–1965), an Italian whose elegant lyricism was much admired in Italian and French roles, but who also did not have a large voice; and Lauritz Melchior (1890–1973), a Dane who became a naturalized American citizen and who was the leading Heldentenor (heroic tenor) of his time (some say of the century), singing mainly Wagnerian roles such as Siegmund, Parsifal, Siegfried, and Tristan, and Verdi's Otello. Melchior, like some other tenors possessing great power and stamina (and like Plácido Domingo), was originally a baritone.

More recently, there have been Richard Tucker (1913–1975), Mario Del Monaco (1915–1982), Franco Corelli (b. 1921), Giuseppe Di Stefano (b. 1921), Carlo Bergonzi (b. 1924), and Nicolai Gedda (b. 1925), all Italians; Alfredo Kraus (b. 1927), a Spaniard; and Jon Vickers (b. 1926), a Canadian.

Within the general tenor category are specific classifications that refer to the tonal quality and degree of power of the singer. The most commonly used are lyric (light), spinto (more powerful), and dramatic (heavy). The term Heldentenor is usually reserved for the tenor of tremendous vocal weight and power who has the physical stamina to last through heavy Wagnerian roles. Tenors rarely if ever fit into just one category; they are constantly crossing the boundary lines.

Before a singer can decide to add a role to his or her repertory, many of its aspects must be considered. The tessitura must fit—not lying too high or too low—and the

Right: The legendary Greek soprano Maria Callas at the Civic Opera House in Chicago, 1958.

type of voice called for in the role, its personality and its color, must be suitable. How the role fits into the singer's performance schedule is another important consideration. For example, as Edward Rothstein detailed in a *New York Times* story in April 1994, "When he [Domingo] sings Parsifal or Siegmund, he is not using the high register much. In an interview for this article, Domingo explained, 'If I am singing after *Parsifal*, it will probably be my best performance of a very high tessitura opera, like *Tales of Hoffmann*, because for a moment I have let the really extreme high part of the voice rest. The best combination, the best medicine for me, is the combination of the repertoire.'"

There are two aspects of vocal color. One may discuss the distinctive color of a particular voice, and then speak about the way that a tenor changes the color of that voice for dramatic purposes within a given role.

Pavarotti's voice is often described as being bright or brilliant, and having "steely brilliance" or "metal," or sounding "metallic." It is also common for Italian voices to be described in terms of the sun or sunshine. Plácido Domingo's voice and those of other Spanish singers are spoken of in terms of being dark and velvety. These basic differences come from the languages themselves, as the sounds of each language are produced by using different combinations of muscles.

The difference between Italian and Spanish tenors was explained by Domingo in a *New York Times* interview in March 1977, to the then *Times* critic Peter G. Davis: "There is a different element in my voice and it is a quality of Spanish singers in general. In Italian tenors the predominant sound is that of metal—bright pinging resonance that can cut through the orchestra like a knife. My voice has more of a cover to it, and the best Spanish voices, if they are well-produced, have more velvet than metal. But velvety voices have a tendency to diminish in projection when they are tired, so I have had to work very hard to build up my velvet to penetrate thicker orchestral sonorities. The secret is to keep the smooth texture, the flexibility, while you develop the power, and I have tried to do this so that my range of roles can be as wide as possible."

Right: Renata Tebaldi, one of the great sopranos of her time, as Tosca. Tebaldi, now retired, was known for the natural beauty of her voice. She rarely sang repertory that was not from her native Italy. After making her debut in 1944, Tebaldi sang at the Metropolitan Opera from 1955 to 1973.

Changing the coloration of one's basic voice is a dramatic technique that everyone—not just singers and actors—uses to convey subtleties of expression and meaning. In opera this is especially important, as the instrumental music may be representing one emotional message and the opera text another, but the subtle coloration of a singer's voice may express yet another emotion or situation. This subtlety of communication adds further depth to the operatic experience.

With time, most voices darken, but the tenor voice probably changes more than others. Even with the natural deepening of the voice, there is no guarantee that all lyric tenors will eventually be able to handle heavy dramatic roles. Some are never able to do so, while others move into the heavier repertory gradually, usually in their mid-thirties to mid-forties.

Opera singing is complex. Excellent breath control is needed to produce what many describe as a column of sound, uniformly strong and focused from top to bottom; there is no weakness or shrillness at the top, nor roughness at the bottom. How a singer negotiates the natural break in the voice, called the "passaggio," between the low and middle registers and between the middle and high registers, is crucial. Daniel Snowman, author of *The World of Plácido Domingo*, likens dealing with the passaggio to working a gear shift. The passaggio can be negotiated smoothly and subtly, with no noticeable switching, say, between the tones of the chest and head voice; or it can be a rough and bumpy dividing line when crossed from either direction. In addition to the technique needed to properly handle this anatomical obstacle, other influential factors can be humidity, barometric pressure, and even how food a singer has eaten has affected him.

Excellent diction is also critical, and uncommon. Singing is a communicative art with music and words intertwined; it makes a huge difference if the singer knows what he is singing about and expresses it effectively.

Above: **The Italian tenor Giovanni Martinelli (center) in the prison scene from Faust.** *Martinelli's remarkable breath control and powerful delivery earned him legendary status in roles such as Otello and Radamès.*

Peter G. Davis, who became music critic of *New York* magazine after leaving *The New York Times*, wrote about a 1992 performance: "....it was a treat to hear singers who, for once, could fit words to notes and understand the connection...."

In a 1973 *Saturday Review* interview by Irving Kolodin, Pavarotti called singing "one of the more difficult forms of muscular activity." Televised opera performances and videos allow audiences to see this for themselves. Close-up shots of singers' heads and faces show the intensity of their physical involvement while whole-body shots reveal the exertion of the work, and of the moment: producing the sound is equally difficult, whether the singer is in his living room or on the stage of the Metropolitan. Added to

this basic physical exertion are the stress and strain of performing a complete work live, in front of major music critics and thousands of discerning listeners who have paid dearly for their tickets, with perhaps a few hundred thousand more people tuned in via live or taped broadcast.

There is not much difference between a professional singer's anatomy and anyone else's. Vocal equipment similar to that of the three tenors can be found in an average person's throat. Dr. Scott M. Kessler is one of the most prominent laryngologists (ear, nose, and throat doctors specializing in the care of the professional voice) in the world. His clients, who see him as much for prevention as for treatment of vocal problems, include some of the biggest names of the opera house and Broadway:

Julie Andrews, Anita Baker, Kathleen Battle, Carol Burnett, Madonna, Sherrill Milnes, Jessye Norman, Samuel Ramey, Beverly Sills, James Taylor, Carol Vanness, and many others.

As Kessler points out, the vocal cords of the three tenors, or of any other performers, are not very distinguished in appearance compared to anyone else's. All vocal cords look very much alike. It is not possible to tell from appearance alone what a person's vocal characteristics might be.

A singer's range, power, and tonal qualities are, like eye color and height, physical attributes with which one is born. They are determined by variables throughout the entire vocal tract, from the diaphragm to the lips and the tip of the nose. Anything that alters the size, shape, or surface conditions of any part of that tract can have great impact on tonal quality and range. The fact that Plácido Domingo is able to do heavy, dramatic Wagnerian parts and Luciano Pavarotti cannot does not make Pavarotti a less great, or weaker, singer. If a singer who is basically a lyric tenor tries to sing a heavier, more dramatic role, he is leaving himself open to the development of nodules, which are calluses that form on the edge of the vocal cords. Singing or speaking lower than one's normal range for an extended period of time will cause this thickening of the skin covering the cords.

The vocal instrument actually goes beyond the voice box to include the lungs below, which produce the air, and the throat, mouth, and nose above, which modify and refine the sound as resonators. The throat is the most passive of the body's sound-producing equipment, being only a passageway. The real power, the full breath support, comes from the upward pressure created by the ribs and the diaphragm muscle.

The actual sound vibrations are created by the vocal cords, two small muscles covered by connective tissue which are situated horizontally in a V-shaped configuration just behind the Adam's apple. The cords open when we breathe, and come together and vibrate when we "phonate"—create a sound by speaking, singing, crying. They are like two blades of grass that, when air is forced between them, will vibrate to produce a sound. Higher tones are produced by the stretching of the cords so that there are thinner bodies to vibrate. Lower tones are produced when the cords are shorter and, therefore, thicker. The vibrations of the cords move out from the center in waves.

The voice box, or larynx, made of cartilage, is not really a box at all, but a triangular cylinder that contains the vocal cords, and the muscles and joints that alter their length and position. It also protects the airway from swallowed food and saliva.

The Adam's apple is the prominent point of cartilage at the front of this area, and protrudes in males more than in females by virtue of the angle and shape of the larynx.

Below: Jon Vickers, at the Metropolitan Opera. Known for his beautiful tone, clear enunciation, and dramatic power, Vickers was one of the great heroic tenors of his generation.

Above: Tenor Beniamino Gigli, at the Metropolitan Opera.

The cords vibrate at a specific frequency, or number of vibrations per second, depending on the pitch we choose to produce. For example, the A to which many orchestras tune vibrates at 440 cycles per second. A person who is singing a tone at this pitch is causing his or her vocal cords to vibrate at the rate of 440 vibrations per second.

The difference between one voice and another, between someone who sounds raspy or flat, and another whose tones are ringing and bell-like, or rich and velvety, depends on the surface conditions of the vocal cords, as well as resonating factors— the shape, structure, and volume of the nasal cavity, and the neuromuscular control of the nasopharynx (the area where the nose and throat connect) and the pharynx (the area and muscles from the roof of the mouth to where you swallow). Vocal quality depends on how these muscles open and close, and how one places the voice (whether the sound will lie within the head or the chest). But a difference can usually be heard if a singer is ill with a cold or flu. Blocked sinuses can make the production of a strong and resonating sound more difficult, thereby creating vocal strain. And if the gelatinous skin surface of the cords is irritated or the cords themselves are swollen, physically creating a sound, beautiful or not, can lead to serious vocal dysfunction.

Vocal problems can be caused by anything that disturbs the evenness of the edge of the vocal cords, or the smoothness of the cords' surface. Nodules, polyps, ruptured blood vessels, and edema (swelling), which often occur with colds or infections, can wreak havoc on the voice, as can fatigue, tension, and virtually any sort of illness. Nodules can be caused by singing with a cold, by misusing the voice (a problem often encountered by rock singers who have not been trained in proper use of the voice), or by smoking or speaking excessively immediately after singing. Permanent damage, though, is unlikely, as professional singers will seek medical attention and/or technical advice as soon as symptoms occur. And it is possible for a singer to recover completely after nodule removal.

Other stresses on the voice come from smoke, air-conditioning, and premenstrual or premenopausal changes. The common denominator of almost all these conditions is a state of reduced hydration, as the vocal cords must have good lubrication to ensure minimum friction. The intake of salt and alcohol, hormonal imbalances (such as elevated estrogen), and even dehydration from exercising can also cause drying of the cords. The ubiquitous glass of water that is never far from any singer in the wings of the stage is like oil for a piece of machinery.

Many myths about singers and singing prevail even in this time of medical sophistication. Body weight, for example, has no bearing on a person's ability to produce a big sound. Vocal power depends only on lung capacity, which remains the same if a person is obese or thin, and on proper breath control.

Most singers are said to be a bit neurotic. It's not easy to have one's instrument inside of one's body. The dependence on the well-being of two small muscles makes every singer's life somewhat precarious. With an opera singer, a case of the sniffles, with the accompanying phlegm and congestion, can become far more than just one person's problem. Finding a substitute for a performance involves a network of administrators, managers, and musicians; canceling one or more performances involves all of those people as well as thousands of audience members who may have to be reimbursed for the cost of their tickets. And of course, the singer who cancels will probably lose his fee. So a bit of neurosis on the part of singers is understandable.

Many professional singers are fearful of drafts and cold temperatures; the year-round wearing of scarves and careful choosing of nondrafty locations in restaurants is common among them. But none of this, according to Dr. Kessler, is medically necessary. Keeping the outside of the neck warm has nothing to do with protecting the voice, or even avoiding a cold; one catches colds only from germs, not from being exposed to cold temperatures.

Left: Jussi Björling as Faust.

Above: Jussi Björling as Rodolfo in Puccini's La Bohème *at the Metropolitan Opera, 1946.*

It is also a myth that sexual abstinence is beneficial to the voice—unless, of course, the singer expresses himself or herself vocally with such intensity during the act that all discipline is lost and the voice is not properly used. But the sexual act itself is not threatening to the singer—unless it poses too much a distraction.

Most singers who get into trouble do so from speaking, not singing. Straining to speak in a noisy room, speaking incorrectly (using the wrong part of the vocal mechanism), or holding a telephone receiver between ear and shoulder (which twists the neck), can be risky. And, although many singers (like Plácido Domingo) abstain from speaking on the day of a performance, Dr. Kessler says that there is no medical reason for doing so, if they use their speaking voices properly. But some singers are most comfortable following this regimen, perhaps as much for its ritualistic or psychological value as for any physical benefits.

It is as reasonable for a singer to take care of his voice as it is for a string player to care for his Stradivarius. The evening before a performance, Plácido Domingo, for example, will vocalize (go through a series of exercises, scales, and repertory excerpts) for about thirty minutes and retire early in order to get ten hours of quality sleep. He prefers to rest his voice, and so will abstain completely from speaking on the day of a performance. That day, after breakfast and a shower, Domingo uses his voice for the first time, vocalizing for about half an hour, which he will do again in his dressing room shortly before the performance. Also, as part of a backstage ritual, Domingo will pray to the patron saint of music, St. Cecilia.

There is good reason for a singer to stay within his or her natural range. By forcing the voice to go unnaturally high or low, a singer physically strains the limits of the cords and can do permanent damage. And undertaking a massive role, such as Otello, if one is not physically suited for it, can bruise and irritate the cords. In most cases, minor damage done by vocal strain can be repaired with two weeks' rest. In some cases prescribed vocal rest can mean no use of the voice at all, not even conversationally.

The aging singer, who can be someone in his or her sixties, seventies, or even eighties, can lose the ability to produce clear and beautiful tones because of wear and tear on the vocal cords and a thickening of the gelatinous surface of the tissues. The vocal cords may lose strength, tension, and endurance, or may become flaccid or "bowed." Lung capacity may be reduced. Loss of the top notes is usually the first sign of problems. Aging singers may no longer be able to sing in tune, as they may not be able to hear themselves as they used to, and are therefore not able to make the tonal adjustments that had always been second nature. Mucus—a beneficial body lubricant in normal amounts—may begin to dry up with age and hormonal changes; tissues begin to atrophy, and breath support can decrease. Certain medications (the use of which usually increases as one ages) can also affect the condition of the vocal cords. But the most important factor in regard to the voice of an aging singer, as with anyone else, is the state of his or her general physical and mental health, which strongly affect each other. Dr. Kessler has seen singers in their seventies who are still performing beautifully, as well as singers in their twenties whose voices have aged beyond repair.

Despite all of his onstage heroics, the tenor is a long-suffering member of the musical community. The good-humored prejudice against tenors makes them the subjects of jokes in which they are profiled as vain, egocentric, and not too bright:

• The beautiful tonal quality of the high tenor voice is due to the empty resonating chamber where brains should be.

• There are men, women, and tenors.

• A tenor, about to take a woman to bed, answers his telephone. "Yes, yes," he replies, then hangs up and says good-bye to his partner, explaining, "I have to sing Tristan in six months."

• A tenor (perhaps the same one, seven months later), in bed with another man's wife, is caught by the husband. "What are you doing?" the husband demands. The tenor sits up: "*Rigoletto* at La Scala, *La Bohème* in Paris...."

In addition to the physical problems faced by singers, their earning power does not usually last as long as that of other professionals; by the age of forty-five, a singer can have his or her career on the decline, to end soon after.

Because of the relative shortage of good tenors, only the best of them are able to command huge fees. Most second-rung tenors earn only respectable, not large, sums. With aging tenors, the first sign of trouble is usually the loss of the "money notes." Is it any wonder then, that tenors are a somewhat nervous group and, therefore, a convenient butt of jokes within the music profession?

Below: Lauritz Melchior, after the final performance of his career. Born in Denmark, and later a naturalized American citizen, Melchior was the most prominent Heldentenor of his time.

Luciano Pavarotti

LUCIANO PAVAROTTI
IS AN UNLIKELY HERO. STANDING
NEARLY AS WIDE AS HE IS TALL, PAVAROTTI
DOES NOT CUT A COMMANDING FIGURE, NOR
IS HIS MANNER NOBLE OR AUSTERE. HE IS

MORE LOVEABLE THAN AWESOME AND APPEALS TO PEOPLE

IN MUCH THE SAME WAY THAT A CHILD DOES: DISARMINGLY UNINHIBITED,

SELF-EFFACING, AND OPENLY CRAVING ATTENTION AND AFFECTION.

Above: Conductor Zubin Mehta and Luciano Pavarotti rehearsing in New York. In the 1990 concert, Mehta matched each singers' enthusiasm and spirit. His contribution to the success of the concert was enormous.
Previous page: Luciano Pavarotti in Houston, 1987. His charismatic personality, in addition to his magnificent voice, has kept him at the forefront of the opera world for decades.

He does, however, have one of the most glorious voices ever heard, and that combination, of the consummate artist inhabiting the body of a teddy bear, has won him a rare status in our society.

Pavarotti is said to be the best-known tenor (or even singer) since Enrico Caruso. But he is probably more famous than Caruso was in his time due to modern technology that can carry a single performance (such as *The 3 Tenors in Concert 1994*) to 1.3 billion people. Today, more people are able to hear Pavarotti in a single television broadcast than could have heard Caruso had he lived several lifetimes.

The Pavarotti that everyone seems to know and love projects a vivid lust for life, enjoying every minute, every note, every bite. Although he inhabits the world of the elite and the intellectual, Pavarotti always seems to be embracing the entire world. He is an interesting combination of The Great Artist and Everyman, with whom everyone can connect if not readily identify.

Some of Pavarotti's detractors say that much of his fame is due to nonoperatic activities, such as his commercials for American Express. Not many opera singers could have done these spots successfully. A haughty artiste would have created a gap between the public and himself

Above: Luciano Pavarotti, 1996.

Above: Pavarotti signs a poster for a fan after the **Three Tenors** *reunion concert, 1994.*

and, therefore, between the public and the product, and the public and the world of opera. Not so—judging from the success of this rotund, bearded broken-English-speaking gentleman's ventures.

Everything about Pavarotti is expansive: his voice, his girth, his gestures, and his concept of musical interpretation. Although he is capable of exquisitely intimate and introspective moments onstage, one thinks of the large statement in connection with this singer.

In public, Pavarotti is almost always "on." He constantly plays to the video and television cameras, poses for the still ones, and performs for whomever might be present. No matter how small or large the crowd, Pavarotti receives his backstage fans—signing autographs, bestowing kisses, and shaking hands—long past any reasonable hour. In a 1980 *Life* magazine interview, his wife of many years, Adua, stated that "the attention is like a drug to him. He likes to feel grand." She explained more in her book, *Pavarotti Life with Luciano*: "I sometimes say, 'It is all the fault of your grandmother,' but really it was the consequences of overindulgence of the male of the species by generations of women before her that I inherited in Luciano....Wherever he is, he is the pivot around which all life revolves." Her husband does not seem to disagree. In a 1976 *Newsweek* article, Pavarotti admitted, "I can't live without applause. It's the oxygen I breathe." Pavarotti is lucky. He needs that adulation and has the ability with which to generate it.

To properly evaluate this voice, one must first peel away a lot of extraneous layers. The various images of the superstar singer—with arms outstretched toward adoring audiences and record buyers, touting the features in television commercials of this expensive watch or that credit card with which to buy it—must be discarded. For behind all of those images is one of the most remarkable voices of our time.

Peter G. Davis' November 1968 *New York Times* review of Pavarotti's Met debut vividly describes the qualities of his voice. The review was entitled, simply, "Luciano Pavarotti, Tenor, Sings Debut at Met in *Bohème*": "Mr. Pavarotti triumphed principally through the natural beauty of his voice—a bright, open instrument with a nice metallic ping up top that warms into an even burnished luster in midrange. Any tenor who can toss off high C's with such abandon, successfully negotiate delicate diminuendo effects and attack Puccinian phrases so fervently is going to win over any *La Bohème* audience and Mr. Pavarotti had them eating out of his hand. As far as acting tenors go, Mr. Pavarotti is not the worst, but his generally stiff and unconvincing stage presence did leave something to be desired."

The most important and unique element in Pavarotti's voice has always been its remarkably beautiful tone, which was never sacrificed even when a good deal of power was put behind it. The voice itself was never very big (which makes his being best known for huge stadium concerts somewhat ironic). Instead, its clear and brilliant quality, consistent from low notes to high, has often been described as being as controlled and focused as a laser beam. But it has always been a laser beam with warmth. A *Time* magazine article in 1979 described the evenness of Pavarotti's notes as "a set of perfectly matched pearls." And his diction has always been superb, with each word perfectly shaped and fitted to the musical line.

Pavarotti's acting ability is generally considered to be the weakest element in his artistry. Bringing a character to life on stage—in opera, theater, or performance art—can happen on many levels. Some singers put more serious thought than others behind their interpretations, giving them a depth of character and psychological complexity that makes the performance all the more revealing. Domingo analyzes a character from all possible perspectives, digging deeply into his psyche, background, and behavior. That character's background, strengths, weaknesses, and motivations all come into play in developing a fully formed characterization. Not so with Pavarotti, whose acting has little character development or depth of interpretation. His dramatics have, on occasion, brought him criticism for overacting. In the grand old Italian operatic tradition, Pavarotti emotes and sobs, arms flung wide in expansive, sometimes clichéd gestures; his portrayals are rarely convincing. Without the instincts of a great actor, or possibly without the insight needed to fully analyze a complex operatic character, Pavarotti always seems

Below: Pavarotti as Riccardo (Gustavus) in the final scene of Verdi's **Un Ballo in maschera** *at the Opéra National de Paris (Opéra Bastille), 1992.*

Above: Opera-star-to-be, Luciano Pavarotti, at age three.

to be Pavarotti, no matter what character he is supposed to be portraying.

Pavarotti was born in Modena, Italy, in 1935. He is said to have been born vocalizing, quickly exhibiting one of the traits for which he would become famous: he had good high notes. Apparently the first music critic he encountered was the doctor who delivered him. "Such high notes!" he reportedly said, as the screaming newborn vocalized at high volume.

Singing in Italy was at that time not limited to the opera house; it was an important part of one's religious life as well. Pavarotti's father was in the chorus at both the opera house and church, and Luciano, while still quite young, joined him to sing in church. Later, in 1955, father and son, as members of the Corale Rossini, the opera chorus, traveled to Llangollen, Wales, for the Royal National Eisteddfod (singing contest). It was the first trip to Britain for both Pavarottis. The choir was one of twenty-two competing from around the world, and they had no expectation of winning, or even of reaching the finals. When all but the Corale Rossini and two other choirs had been disqualified, the young Luciano is said to have passed out, apparently in a state of nervousness approaching hysteria—or so the story goes. He was revived in time for the choir to be awarded the top prize.

This was the first evidence that Luciano might have wanted a future as a professional musician. Two years earlier, before the scope of his musical ability began to become apparent, and in spite of his love for singing, Luciano had decided to become a teacher, completing the necessary two-year training course. Pavarotti's girlfriend,

Adua, had worked in a local elementary school, hence his decision. It was immediately obvious that he was not a natural teacher, as Pavarotti recounted in his autobiography, *Pavarotti My Own Story* (written with William Wright): "I would like to be able to say I adored my students and they adored me, but it was not like that. They were absolutely wild, screaming all the day. I did not have the authority of a regular teacher and the little monsters did whatever they felt like. I wanted to kill every one of them. I think I would love to teach, but in an orderly, systematic way. Not like that. I did it for about two years while I was studying voice. It was a terrible experience."

It is interesting to note that Pavarotti, whenever asked about what he will do when he is no longer able to sing, expresses a desire to teach young singers, perhaps to ensure that the great tradition of the opera will continue, and perhaps to ensure that he will have a meaningful, substantial role in it. Pavarotti occasionally conducts master classes at conservatories such as The Juilliard School in New York. These sessions involve advanced, talented students who may be within a few years of having professional careers. But master classes are one-time events, with little chance of ongoing instruction. And with famous musicians such as Pavarotti, large audiences and members of the media are often present, precluding any chance of real communication between student and teacher.

While master classes can convey basic insight into a student's technique and musical approach, as well as some practical secrets of the trade, they are very different from working closely and in depth with a student over a period of years. It is the more substantial, long-term, intimate relationship that truly nurtures the student musician, and allows the teacher to influence every facet of his or her musical development.

Pavarotti has already made substantial efforts to ease the way for future singers. Wanting to mark Pavarotti's longtime association with the Opera Company of Philadelphia, the company started a competition in his honor in 1980, to be held every four years. Called the Opera Company of Philadelphia/Luciano Pavarotti International Voice Competition, it has given many aspiring young singers the opportunity to showcase their talent. Pavarotti suggested the idea for the competition; it was his way of giving something back to the profession and the art. The Opera Company of Philadelphia had their fourth, and last, competition in 1992. The contest is now administered by Tibor Rudas, the master producer behind Pavarotti's, and the Three Tenors', stadium concerts. Pavarotti has donated all of his services to this cause, including singing the lead in the operatic performance that showcases each competition's winners. In 1986, the winners were lucky enough to sing in a performance of *La Bohème* with Pavarotti in mainland China.

In spite of his bad teaching experience, Pavarotti had become popular with his students' families, and these connections provided a rich source of potential clients for a new line of work: selling insurance policies. Pavarotti was a convincing and appealing salesman, and he did well. Perhaps too well. The constant talking essential to selling insurance was wearing on his voice. Around 1960, he decided to sacrifice the financial security of being a salesman for the intense studying and hard work of building a professional singing career.

Even for a talent like Pavarotti's, success would take time. But he had the emotional support of his fiancée, Adua, and the financial support of his family, who agreed to help him until he was thirty. After that, if Pavarotti was not able to make his way as a professional musician, he would consider another line of work.

Pavarotti's singing was limited to small productions in nearby towns. He became increasingly discouraged and depressed, and described his singing at one event in Ferrara as "a baritone who was being strangled." He decided to give up singing completely. As is often the case with such decisions, the sudden lessening of pressure released a great deal of energy. During what Pavarotti thought would be his "farewell concert at the age of twenty-five," he thrilled both the audience and himself with the sounds for which he would soon become famous. He had crossed the line from being a promising young talent to a committed artist.

The musical work necessary to build a singing career has never been a hardship for Pavarotti. Even the endless, repetitious vocal exercises that build a singer's technique have always been enjoyable to him, from the time of his youth.

Pavarotti's big break came in 1961, at age twenty-six, when he won the Achille Peri competition for young

singers. First prize was a professional engagement as Rodolfo in *La Bohème* with the opera company in nearby Reggio Emilia.

Every successful career has its share of luck to add to talent and hard work; in Pavarotti's case, luck had it that one of his fellow cast members was the bass Dmitri Nabokov, son of the writer Vladimir Nabokov, whose book *Lolita* was causing a stir at the time. An important agent from Milan, Alessandro Ziliani, had come to hear the young Nabokov and, with a keen ear for music and a good nose for business, realized that it was the young Pavarotti who could have the career. This agent worked with Pavarotti over the next few years, helping him make the correct early moves that are so critical to a major career. Another bit of good fortune was that *La Bohème*'s conductor, Francesco Molinari-Pradelli, was a major

Above: Fernando Pavarotti and his son, Luciano, singing in church. The elder Pavarotti, according to his son, has an excellent voice. Extreme nervousness before performances prevented him from considering a professional career.

Above: Australian soprano Joan Sutherland played opposite Pavarotti in Lucia di Lammeroor *in 1965.*

performances (as they do today), scouting for young talent. It took four months for Pavarotti to see the result of Ingpen's visit. When Giuseppe Di Stefano became incapacitated, Pavarotti was called on to sing Rodolfo in Covent Garden's *La Bohème*. The next day's review in the *London Times* proclaimed the "Discovery of Great New Italian Tenor."

Joan Ingpen also introduced Pavarotti to Joan Sutherland, one of the great sopranos of her time, and Richard Bonynge, her conductor husband. Because of the quality of Pavarotti's voice, he would be an excellent musical partner for Sutherland. In addition, his height (at nearly six feet) made him a suitable dramatic partner for the tall soprano as well. Pavarotti was immediately engaged for a fourteen-week tour of Australia with Sutherland and Bonynge in 1965. Singing in *Lucia di Lammermoor*, *La Sonnambula*, *La Traviata*, and *L'Elisir d'amore*, Pavarotti had the chance to observe Sutherland closely. He soon realized that the foundation of her extraordinary sound was her remarkable breathing technique. Apparently Sutherland did not mind having Pavarotti's hand frequently on her diaphragm, investigating how she took in her reservoir of air, harnessed the power of its force, and used specific muscles as machinery to do so. It was from Sutherland that Pavarotti learned many of the great early lessons of his art.

The next big break came in 1967, when Pavarotti was invited to sing in the Verdi *Requiem* at La Scala. Pavarotti had sung at that revered house only sporadically, appearing more often at the Vienna Staatsoper, which had a reciprocal agreement with La Scala whereby singers moved between the two houses as needed, mainly filling in during emergency situations. The conductor in Vienna, Herbert von Karajan, one of the most important and powerful maestros in the world, had been impressed with Pavarotti's work, having conducted him in two performances of *La Bohème* in 1965. The 1967 La Scala Verdi *Requiem* was a memorial concert in honor of Arturo Toscanini, marking the tenth anniversary of his death. As guest conductor of this event, von Karajan was able to invite the singers of his choice, and to be invited by him was very impressive. To sing in what is considered the foremost opera house in the world, in one of Verdi's greatest works, in honor of the most venerated Italian

musical figure who provided additional opportunities for the young singer. While Pavarotti's story is not one of rags-to-riches, it was a classic launching of a career, and one that would provide a strong foundation for one of longevity and substance.

With his singing career underway, Pavarotti married Adua on September 30, 1961, and the first of their three daughters made her debut not long after.

During the next two years, Pavarotti learned four or five roles. While performing *Rigoletto* in Dublin in 1963, he was heard by Joan Ingpen, at that time casting director of the Royal Opera House, Covent Garden. It was not just good luck that she was in the audience but a natural and expected occurrence in a blossoming career. Pavarotti was now making the rounds of the smaller opera houses, and representatives of the major houses frequently attended conductor in modern history, with one of the most highly respected conductors of the time, made this one of those musical events that was important to both the general public and to the music profession. It was also one of those musical events which can put a young singer on the international map.

Less than a year later, Pavarotti's performance in *La Bohème* in San Francisco won him an invitation to make his debut in the same opera at the Metropolitan Opera the following year, starring with a lifelong friend, Mirella Freni, also a native of Modena. (As infants, Pavarotti and Freni had shared a wet nurse, and Freni took every opportunity to joke about who, obviously, had gotten most of the milk.)

The importance of a Met debut, for a major talent, cannot be overstated. By the time of a debut, the opera world will have been talking for months about the singer's characteristics—the type, weight, and color of his voice—and his acting ability, diction, and physique. His strengths and weaknesses in all of these areas are fair game for debate. His management and publicity representatives will have been working hard to stir up excitement without hyping the singer to the point where there will be a back-lash from audience and critics. Record company executives will be in attendance, as will everyone else in the business: they either want to show off their own connection to the new talent or see what their own clients will be competing against. The public will come out of curiosity and hope: will this singer continue the great tradition of the Met, and of opera in general? Will he be the one to guarantee a new Golden Age of opera? Will he enliven and enrich their lives? And the critics will be out in force, either to point out how wrong everyone else has been, or to prove that they are astute enough to know, early on, that this new talent will have a life of his or her own.

So here was young Pavarotti, thirty-two years old, fully prepared in every way to make his Met debut but coming down with the flu. Desperate not to cancel, he decided instead to postpone the debut by a week. He was able to sing the first performance with some degree of critical success. In spite of his illness, Pavarotti's reviews were "respectable" (his description), but he knew that he had not sung to his full potential. He could not continue past the second act of the second performance. He

Above: Pavarotti as Nemorino in Donizetti's L'Elisir d'amore *at the Metropolitan Opera, 1989.*

Above: **A young Luciano (left) on stage with Sutherland and Spiro Malas in Donizetti's La Fille du regiment** *at Covent Garden Opera House, 1972.*

and made most performers seem ten pounds heavier than they actually were. Close-ups of faces and bodies could work against the drama's effectiveness if a singer's physical features were not true to that of the character.

Pavarotti, however, seemed to be exempt from this. His huge size not only never seemed to hurt his career, it seemed to work in his favor. It became, in effect, part of the lore and the legend. Even though there were parts he could not, as an overweight man, play convincingly, he was more often described as loveable and cuddly than fat. His love of food and his habit of overeating were not discussed as symptoms of neuroses but as charming personality quirks to be exploited in the press. It was all used as blocks in building a towering public persona.

One publicizable aspect of Pavarotti's career and life was used to feed another. Because of the financial success that resulted from his

cancelled the remaining Met performances to rush to his sickbed at home in Modena, where he remained for almost three months.

Pavarotti was invited back to the Met for performances as Alfredo in *La Traviata* in 1970, but it was not until 1972 and his *La Fille du régiment* performances with Joan Sutherland, when he took all nine high Cs in one aria, that he had his great triumph. The audience went wild, the critics raved, and the media reported it all. In one evening, Pavarotti had come to be recognized worldwide. His career was now moving ahead on its own steam.

Years ago, the opera singer, in generic images, was always pictured as rotund. Many thought wrongly that obesity was essential to the production of a large sound. Television changed much of that. As opera broadcasts became more plentiful, singers who were attractive in addition to having beautiful voices saw their careers progress. Television cameras brought the audience right up onstage

fame, he could afford to indulge himself, and even these indulgences became newsworthy. Pavarotti was the first Western person to sing in Beijing's Great Hall of the People in Communist China, where he performed before a sold-out audience of ten thousand in 1986. Although he planned to try some of the local cuisine, he did not want to take any chances that his beloved Italian food would not be available when he wanted it. His plane took off from Genoa laden with pasta, veal, fresh vegetables, fruit, olive oil, fine Italian cheeses, and ten kilos of Genovese basil sauce. And the essential equipment was there to go with it: refrigerators, hot plates, and cooking utensils. Pavarotti was not left to his own culinary devices with all of this; two noted restauranteurs from Genoa accompanied the Pavarotti family, custom-cooking their meals in the Beijing hotel. It was not quite as romantic as it may sound, at least for Luciano's wife, Adua: "For several nights I clambered over crates of tortellini and slept surrounded by aubergines and jars of olives, the air heavy with the smell of rotting melons."

So, where another singer of Pavarotti's girth might be criticized for overindulgence, he became all the more famous because of it. Not every singer could afford to transport favorite foods, equipment, and chefs. But for Pavarotti, this expense provided additional grist for the publicity mill, and therefore boosted his career and his income. And when Pavarotti decided to diet, that became newsworthy as well. The media reported that the Metropolitan Opera's wardrobe staff had to take in Pavarotti's *Il Trovatore* costumes a minimum of six inches and recipes of his favorite diet foods were published in newspapers.

Despite being a citizen of the world (Pavarotti travels constantly; out of a full calendar year, he spends all but about a month traveling between opera companies, concerts, and recording sessions), he has always maintained a loving closeness to his hometown of Modena, in north central Italy. It is there that he has always lived. He also maintains an apartment in New York, where one of the principal features is a large, specially designed kitchen. Pavarotti likes his creature comforts and is able to have them.

The house in Modena that Luciano and Adua acquired in 1978 satisfied his longtime desire to bring together the immediate family from both sides. This huge property, resembling a compound, allowed the Pavarottis to have the main house for themselves, a separate flat for Adua's sister and her family, a separate building for Luciano's parents, his sister, and her son, and others as well. More than twenty members of the extended Pavarotti family have been in residence there at one time or another.

But being a member of the Pavarotti family is not all pleasure. As with the families of many

celebrities, it is difficult for them to have a normal life when Pavarotti is present. Meals in restaurants are interrupted by strangers' requests for handshakes and autographs; the enjoyment of an evening at the theater or movies is disrupted by whispering and pointing; and, as Adua relates in her book, even time at home is pressured by "visitors arriving and departing, by the telephone ringing, and by the constant activity that surrounds him wherever he is."

For most stars, always on the go, there is the stress of long waits in airport lounges, canceled flights, and missed connections. Pavarotti, with his fame and fortune, often has specially arranged flights and VIP treatment at airports, but there still can be lonely nights in strange hotels, meals eaten on the run, packing and unpacking. It all takes its toll. In the case of an opera singer, the situation can be even more difficult. Late night socializing, which might be professionally necessary, is difficult before a day of early rehearsals. And if bad weather prevails, a singer

Below: Pavarotti and Adua are toasted at a book signing at Harrods of London.

Above: (left to right) The Pavarotti family: Adua, daughter Giuliana, Papà, daughters Cristina and Lorenza.
Right: Pavarotti with companion Nicoletta Mantovani.

will rarely risk catching a sore throat or virus, opting instead to stay indoors, alone, sometimes for days at a time. It can be a lonely life, away from one's family, as Pavarotti himself recounts, unsure of who one's friends really are. "They [my friends] tell me, 'There are many people who want to take advantage of you, who want to make use of your friendship.' Maybe there are, but I cannot live my life like that—mistrusting everyone. I am not naive. I know that I have friends who are friends mainly because I am a famous singer. That is not to say they don't like me. I think they do, but I know that when I lose my voice, they may not be friends any more. I will call them and they will be busy. But I am philosophical about that. I don't mind. It is just the way things are."

But Pavarotti revealed a basic loneliness to Will Crutchfield in a 1985 *New York Times* interview. "Little by little the music takes the place of a certain kind of affection or company. There," Pavarotti said, pointing to the big black piano where he does his *lavoro* [work], "there is my friend."

It does not seem, however, to be his only friend. There was a great deal of publicity in February 1996, when, after some thirty-five years of marriage, Pavarotti confirmed rumors of his romantic involvement with his secretary, Nicoletta Mantovani. At age twenty-six, she was younger than all of Pavarotti's three daughters. The two had been seen together in Barbados. *People Weekly*, in its March 11, 1996, issue, noted that the Italian magazine *Chi* had published pictures of the two kissing. Pavarotti was quoted as telling the magazine, "To hide it would be a crime. She is

my favorite of my harem." Mantovani, the magazine said, was a Bologna-born former forest ranger who was hired to work for Pavarotti in 1992. After years of rampant rumors of her husband's infidelity (and after more than thirty-six years of marriage), Adua Pavarotti, insiders say, is considering filing for divorce.

Such activities outside of the opera house have created a good deal of criticism for Pavarotti, as have his television specials, product endorsements, and blatant use of publicity. Sharing the blame for this is his manager, Herbert Breslin, the mastermind behind the publicity machine. But his public image seems to be somewhat different from who he really is. The secure and confident person might not really exist.

While many people have labeled Pavarotti's ubiquitous handkerchief a prop and a gimmick, Pavarotti calls it "my security blanket." This challenges the enduring myth that celebrities are somehow exempt from the emotional insecurities that plague others. They are thought of as

Above: In China, in 1986, Pavarotti drew the capacity crowds and enthusiastic ovations that he attracts everywhere in the world. With trademark handkerchief in hand, he acknowledged the cheers of the audience after his first concert in that country, at the Peking Exhibition Center.

superhuman—confident onstage and offstage, comfortable both as the center of attention in Carnegie Hall and as a guest in someone's home. But some celebrities are so insecure on a one-to-one basis that they may not be comfortable carrying on a normal conversation. And to others, the fear of performing may be an almost paralyzing sensation.

Pavarotti says that he began to carry the handkerchief to prevent himself from gesturing too much while singing, and it has become a comfort to him as well. He explained in his autobiography how the attachment to the piece of white cloth began. "It was with my second concert, in Dallas, that I took up the habit of carrying a large white handkerchief. I know it looks silly in some ways, like those old divas who used to carry a fichu. I use it, actually, to make myself look *less* silly. I went to a concert given by a colleague of mine and found myself horrified by the way my friend in every aria gesticulated wildly and pranced around. He looked like a crazy man. I decided I must do something to prevent myself from getting carried away like that. By holding the white handkerchief, I keep myself more in one spot. If I were to start making large gestures, the handkerchief would fly all over the place and catch my attention like a warning flag. Then, too, I have gotten used to it now and it relaxes me. It is my security blanket while on the concert stage."

His need for a security blanket seems understandable. In a 1994 television conversation with Charlie Rose, Pavarotti admitted (in his own brand of English), that he never feels confident: "...nobody feels comfort in our profession." Rose asked about his feelings ten minutes before a performance. "Awful," Pavarotti responded. "Horrendous....When you go out, you and your voice, and you hear then your partner, who is your voice, is answering very well to you, you become another person."

He also admitted, "I am always nervous before a performance. Any singer who says he is not is lying." He went as far as to call his taking his position on stage a "death march."

Apparently security blankets are not quite enough. To deal with personal insecurities, the lack of control over a

bit of phlegm on the vocal cords, and the changing tides of audience loyalty, Pavarotti (as is the European custom) depends on *un chiodo curvo*, a bent nail in his pocket, which he must find just before a performance begins. He detailed his ritual in *Pavarotti My Own Story*, "As we enter the stage area, I search for my bent nail. This is a superstition I have had for years. I don't like to sing until I have found a bent nail on the stage floor. Usually, it is not that difficult with all the carpentry done backstage. The belief is a combination of two Italian superstitions—metal for good luck and bent to suggest the horns that ward off evil....The habit makes Adua angry because later I put the nail in my pocket and it often tears a hole which she must have repaired." Pavarotti knows that many nails that have ended up in his possession have been planted by sympathetic stagehands, but it does not matter; their power will be intact, no matter what their origin.

Pavarotti's superstition is not limited to bent nails. His wife writes that he always takes the same route and tries to stay in the same hotels, fearing that change might bring bad luck. But tradition and superstition have always been part of theater life.

One wonders if Pavarotti had a bent nail in his possession in 1969, when an earthquake struck while he was onstage in a San Francisco Opera production of *La Bohème*. In a 1979 article on the tenor, *Time* magazine reported that Pavarotti "gripped the hand of his Mimi, Dorothy Kirsten, a little more tightly, but kept on singing at full voice and never missed a beat. The earthquake drew to a peaceful conclusion and so did the performance."

Some of Pavarotti's problems could have been solved not by bent nails but by better judgement. In 1992, in a concert in Modena involving several artists, Pavarotti was caught lip-synching to one of his

Below: September, 1995, Pavarotti escorts the late Princess Diana through his hometown of Modena, Italy.

own recordings rather than singing live like everyone else. He explained that he had not had time to rehearse.

Then, in 1993, there was another question of credibility. When Pavarotti sang the role of the painter Cavaradossi in *Tosca* in Chicago in 1976, a fan sent him a set of oil paints. Pavarotti began to paint for relaxation but soon found it so involving that it became almost an obsession. Because he was Pavarotti, the hobby did not stay on that level; a Milan gallery began to represent him, organizing exhibitions that were coordinated with his opera performances. His paintings and silk-screen works, very much in the primitive style, sold for big bucks. In 1993, the *Los Angeles Times* reported that not all of the paintings were Pavarotti originals but had been copied from a how-to-paint book called *My Adventures in Europe* by Mary E. Hicks, at that time an eighty-seven-year-old Californian who was living on Social Security. Mrs. Hicks did not rush to sue, nor did she ask for an apology. She wanted only recognition that Pavarotti's paintings were really her creations. She received this recognition when, in true Pavarotti fashion, the news was carried by publications from the *New York Times* to *Artnews*.

Pavarotti's credibility also seems weakened by persistent rumors about an inability to read music. His detractors raise this issue as often as they can, but it is not as important as it may seem to be. By knowing a role inside out, and by working with a fine vocal coach, a singer who cannot read musical notation can still be able to deliver a high-quality performance. It may not have the type of depth and character development that one by, say, Domingo might have, but the performance will have other qualities that are equally valid, and will suit the personality of the singer. If such rumors are true, this deficiency has certainly not prevented Pavarotti from delivering some of the most memorable performances in modern history.

Pavarotti is a survivor. In addition to crises of credibility, there have been physical and emotional ones as well. Perhaps he had his bent nails handy in 1975 when he survived an airplane crash at a Milan airport. Landing in poor weather conditions, the plane skidded off the runway and broke in two. In the terrifying blackness of night, Pavarotti escaped unharmed. The crash was, in a way, a gift. Pavarotti had been going through an uncharacteristic period of depression. As he described in his autobiogra-

phy, it was not severe "but might as well have been, it was so unshakable....I was also upset, I know, about my weight. I was very fat and I felt this was seriously hurting my career. In my profession I felt pushed aside, dismissed—and I disliked myself very much for growing so fat....The entire airplane crash experience was as though God had grabbed me by the neck and said, 'You are so indifferent about life? Here, take a look at death and tell me how you like that!' If that was His plan, it worked....Since that accident, I have been optimistic and happy, perhaps more so than ever. Because of the terrible things I saw during the war, because of [a] near-fatal illness as a boy, and then the crash at the Milan airport, I think I know death. I also know life—I know as well as anyone how precious and beautiful it is."

One might think that, given his share of fame and fortune, Pavarotti holds an enviable position of independence. But it is not quite that simple. In a *Life* magazine interview in 1980, Pavarotti admitted that "...the public is my boss. It is the price you pay." Indeed, it is the public whom he must keep happy. It is they who buy records and videos and tickets to his concerts, and they who tune in to his television broadcasts.

Pavarotti's dependence on the public includes another, substantial, aspect. "I am a very loving person and I need lots of love," he writes. "There is something very special

Above: Pavarotti with one of his canvases. Painting proved to be a relaxing and engaging hobby for him, but also got him into trouble with charges of plagiarism.

Above: Tenor Pavarotti with baritone Frank Sinatra, two singers who rose to the tops of their respective performance fields.

A singer's equipment is fragile and cannot be abused. By singing roles that are too high or too low, serious and permanent damage to the voice may be done. In the early nineties, Pavarotti, always clearly a lyric tenor, tried to push his limits to include the heavier dramatic works. Some singers, with the natural darkening and deepening of the voice that occur with age, are able to move into these roles. But Pavarotti's voice was always so completely that of a lyric tenor that it was not good judgement for him to have given in to such temptation, and some critics feel that his voice did not respond well to the stress of singing these roles. His attempt to sing Otello, the great Verdi role that is the pinnacle for dramatic tenors, in Carnegie Hall with conductor Georg Solti in 1991, was not successful (Pavarotti claimed that the poor quality of his singing was due to a cold). He attempted other roles such as Radamès, for which his voice also was basically unsuited. After this, his exquisite tone sometimes sounded strained, and his extraordinary high notes were not always there. In 1995, some twenty-two years after his historic nine high Cs in *La Fille du régiment*, Pavarotti tried the role again, this time missing the first of the notes—to gasps from the audience—then sang the rest of the aria down an octave. In his defense, Pavarotti said that there was phlegm on his vocal cords, but it is doubtful that vocal cords belonging to any sixty year-old tenor could successfully negotiate those high Cs.

Pavarotti, as his wife has written, likes to be in control. He makes decisions and his orders are followed. But there will come a time, which some say is near, when he will order his vocal cords to vibrate and they will not obey, at least not in the way that they have for most of his life. They will no longer vibrate at exactly the right frequencies, nor will his lungs create the perfect column of air. His tones will not reach high into that thrilling stratosphere of sound that is at once superhuman yet seems as inevitable as an element of nature, and his hearing may no longer be able to detect right notes from wrong. Whether he will have the wisdom and courage, as some but not all singers have, to put the art first and step down from the stage, or whether he will continue to perform as long as there are audience members in front of him, no one knows. His psychological need to perform may not diminish at the same rate as his physical ability. The implications of retirement

about the love an audience gives you. It is not like any other. With your friends and your family, you can never be sure how much they love you or if the love will last. There are so many complicated reasons for the love between individuals. But between a performer and the audience, it is not complicated. It is very simple. If they love you, they tell you; if they don't, they will not pretend. What is more, as long as you perform as they wish you to, they are willing to tell you every night."

Since the seventies, Pavarotti's fame has enabled him to give solo concerts in addition to opera performances. These "one-man shows," which are usually performed in partnership with a pianist, pay many times more than opera performances but are demanding in very different ways. Of the pressures of solo concerts, Pavarotti writes, "Vocally, it was much more work than singing an opera— and no one ever said that singing an opera was easy. You have no rest periods when others carry the evening, no one to console the audience if you are not in top form, no other element—sets, costumes, dancers, other singers—to divert them from your weaknesses. It is the ultimate test for the singer—the *mano a mano* of the vocal world."

Above: Luciano Pavarotti, **Concert at Central Park,** *1993.*

Right: Pavarotti played an opera star in love with an American woman in the 1982 film, **Yes, Giorgio.**

presence of royalty, aristocracy, and large numbers of common folk, was televised live by satellite to thirty-three countries. Pavarotti has filled New York's Central Park with his sound and a half million fans. His concerts at Madison Square Garden were record breakers, and he has even performed in Las Vegas and at the Foxwoods Resort Casino, where a bingo hall was transformed into a concert hall. These mega-concerts bring Pavarotti great exposure as well as the largest fees of any artist in classical music.

Like such predecessors as basso Ezio Pinza and tenor Mario Lanza, who expanded their popularity mainly through radio and movies, Pavarotti, too, followed the beckoning of the silver screen to star in a movie, an ill-begotten film called *Yes, Georgio* that was made in 1982. The film took thirteen weeks to shoot and cost $21 million. It was reviewed unfavorably by the *Village Voice*'s Leighton Kerner in a critique titled "No, Giorgio."

But while the movie was short-lived, virtually everything else that Pavarotti has done will be handed down to posterity. The technology of our age means that Pavarotti's singing has a life beyond the walls of the concert hall. In addition to television and radio broadcasts, there are CDs, CD ROMs, home videos, and laser disks available that will capture his performances for present fans as well as for generations to come.

from the stage are certainly great for him, but are also great for his fans. There will be a significant gap in their lives, too.

But Pavarotti's fans are fortunate because of all the exposure their hero has had. Pavarotti has starred in both prime-time commercial and public television specials, and has been joined on television—and in live benefits—by the likes of Frank Sinatra, Loretta Lynn, and Carol Burnett.

In 1990, only Madonna and Elton John sold more recordings worldwide than Luciano Pavarotti. More than 50 million copies of his albums and videos have been sold to date, and there is no end in sight. All of his "stadium" concerts have been performed in front of massive audiences, with most being televised and/or taped for eventual home video release.

In addition to the extraordinary 1990 *Three Tenors* concert in Rome, his 1991 Hyde Park Concert, in the

Plácido Domingo

A *New York Times Magazine* article by Gerald Walker discussed Plácido Domingo's incessant mix of performing, traveling, studying, recording, and promoting his career, and raised the reasonable concern that Domingo may be in danger of burning himself out. That article appeared in 1972, when Domingo was just thirty-one!

Above: Plácido Domingo, one third of The Tenors, performing at the Dodger Stadium concert, Los Angeles, 1994.
Previous page: Plácido Domingo, receiving France's decoration of the Légion d'Honneur.

Another article, in the *New York Post* by Fern Marja Eckman, stated much the same concern: "He has blanketed the operatic scene in so unprecedented a fashion that colleagues and critics fear his voice—big, beautiful, like molten gold from the top to bottom of his register—will burn itself out before he is too much older." This was in 1977, when he was thirty-six.

Since then, Domingo has not only maintained that level of activity but has increased it, taking on conducting and administrative responsibilities. Still going strong at an age when most singers are beginning to think about retirement, he is now becoming as well known for his longevity as for his prolific output and high quality.

Domingo's appetite for making music seems to be insatiable. Born in Madrid in 1937, his professional singing career began around 1959 when he auditioned for the Mexican National Opera as a baritone and was accepted as a tenor. That career has not waned. Between 1959 and 1996 (according to the November 1996 *New York Times* article "A High-Voltage Dynamo Named Domingo"), he has squeezed in 2,700 performances in more than 109 operatic roles, made ninety-three recordings of sixty-two operas, and filmed more than fifty music videos—not counting the Three Tenors concerts. It is probable that no other opera singer in history has done as much as he.

He is ubiquitous. In addition to his singing engagements, he has signed a four-year contract to be artistic director of the Washington Opera, starting with the 1996–97 season; serves as artistic adviser and principal guest conductor of the Los Angeles Music Center Opera, having started there in 1995; has regularly appeared in traditionally nonoperatic settings, such as the Macy's Thanksgiving Day Parade and the 1996 Yankees' World Series victory celebration (where he sang "Take Me out to the Ball Game" with Robert Merrill); and conducts symphonic (nonoperatic) concerts with major orchestras.

It is remarkable not only that Domingo is physically able to do all this—that he has the stamina and that his vocal equipment is still in good shape—but that he is able to do it all so well. After decades of singing, which causes wear and tear on the voice, there is no sign of his voice giving way to use or age. The freshness is mostly there, and he is still able to sing the roles of virile young heroes

Above: Domingo has added the role of conductor to his long list of talents and activities. He has made the remarkable statement that he regards himself as a natural conductor, more than a natural singer.

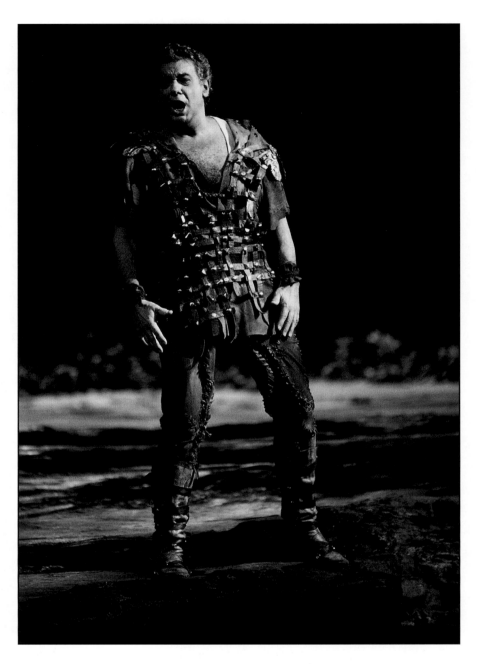

Above: Plácido Domingo as Siegmund in the Metropolitan Opera's **Die Walküre.** *Domingo was able to move successfully into the Wagnerian repertory, which demands great stamina, in addition to great musicianship.*

vocal cords are made out of the same stuff as those of other singers.

One would think that the term "musical" could be applied to every accomplished musician, but what it is used to connote is much too rare for that. It refers to an innate, natural ability to express one's self through music, going beyond just the ability to play an instrument well or to sing well. Many highly successful professional musicians have great technical facility and can move their listeners deeply. But it can be a highly cultivated ability, not deeply intuitive. Baseball icon Pete Rose referred to the difference between natural and cultivated ability when he explained that he was not a naturally great ball player: he had to work hard at it. This does not mean that natural talents do not have to work hard. But the effort is needed more for technical accomplishment than the interpretative or the expressive.

Without this musicality, or strong musical instinct, a performance would be merely an empty show of technique, an uncommunicative exercise. If any deficiency must exist, many feel it should involve the technique and not the communicative qualities. As pianist Arthur Rubinstein, one of the great musical communicators, used to say, "It is better to play the wrong notes right than the right notes wrong."

The responsibility, however, may not lie exclusively with the person onstage. All performers are influenced by the reaction of their audiences. Pavarotti has commented that his voice seems to open and bloom when he is in front of a particularly receptive group. But it's very difficult to know which comes first, the good audience or the involving performer. Musical entertainer and pianist Victor Borge has said that no audience comes to the theater wanting to have a bad time, so it would stand to reason that a group of people who have paid for their tickets, have given up an evening or afternoon, and have taken the trouble to travel to the hall, must want to enjoy themselves. Is it, therefore, always the fault of the performer if an evening goes flat? Perhaps it has something to do with the phase of the moon or barometric pressure or the health of the stock market that day, but it is a partnership, and is one of the mysteries of live performance.

Some musicians are so innately musical that this characteristic imbues every musical utterance and gesture.

convincingly. For some reason, the rules that apply to other singers do not seem to apply to him. "The more I sing," he has said on many occasions, "the better I sound." And where careful but frequent use is wonderful for string instruments and the best pianos, the opposite tends to be true for the human voice. Use it carefully, or it may not last. Do not sing too much without giving the voice, as well as the body, a good rest. This is true except when it pertains to Domingo's voice. One begins to wonder if his

Their ability and need to express themselves musically are not limited just to their own instruments; hand them another and they will be able to make some meaningful musical utterance. Chances are that they showed this talent as youngsters: their mealtime place settings became percussion sections, and empty boxes resonated with the rhythms of small hands.

Plácido Domingo is one such musician. Innately musical, he instinctively knows and feels the underlying line and pulse within an operatic part, understands where it fits harmonically and melodically within the total score, and what its relationship is to the other singers' and to the orchestra's parts. He is able to get inside the composer's skin and, therefore, help to communicate what the creator intended.

Domingo's musicality allows him to recover easily from a conductor's incorrect cue or a colleague's missed line. He knows instinctively whether to keep singing or whether to stop, and if he does continue, where to pick up the line effectively. This kind of instinct can save a performance from collapse—from orchestra players going in one direction and singers in another. When such a recovery is done with subtlety and smoothness, an audience may never know that disaster was only an eighth note away.

Another aspect of Domingo's natural musicality is his ability to teach himself new roles. The great majority of opera singers must rely on coaches who act as guides to the work in preparation, explaining how the part should be approached, and the kinds of vocal techniques that should be used. Domingo is a very good pianist who can negotiate his way through the most complex scores. He has the rare ability to take a full orchestral score, which contains every note played by every member of the orchestra, and "reduce it" for the two hands of a pianist. By doing this, he is able to see how his operatic part fits into the totality with the orchestra and the other singers' parts. Since Domingo does not need an intermediary, his interpretation of a role is not filtered through someone else's influences or biases. This is not to say, however, that other singers who do not have Domingo's musical or pianistic abilities are at an artistic disadvantage. A singer of excellence (and intelligence), working with a knowledgeable and insightful coach, can deliver brilliant technical and interpretive performances.

Domingo brings both instinct and insight to the characters he plays. In a 1982 *Newsweek* article, "Bravissimo, Domingo!," he shared his thinking about Otello, his digging beneath the surface to understand the complexity of the Moor: "Otello is not brutal," Domingo related, "the way many people portray him. He is a great warrior, but as a human being he is naive." Domingo's preparation for such roles does not end with his own analysis. He has revealed that, for his Otello performances, he not only listens to the interpretations of other opera singers but is

Above: Domingo in the title role in Verdi's Otello, *Metropolitan Opera, 1994. Verdi's penultimate opera was written when he was in his seventies. A masterpiece, the work demands vocal strength and beauty, physical stamina, and the ability to portray the character with insight and understanding.*

Right: *Plácido Domingo as Otello, a role that to many is the most demanding of all parts in the tenor repertory. In addition to singing the role magnificently, Domingo brings a depth of character to the role that earned him the praises of the late actor Sir Laurence Olivier, whose performances of Shakespeare's* Othello *were considered to have set the standard.*

influenced by actors such as the late Laurence Olivier and Orson Welles. Olivier once returned the compliment. "You realize," he told the movie and opera director Franco Zeffirelli, "that Domingo plays Othello as well as I do, and he has that voice."

In addition to Domingo's fine acting instincts, he is physically able to accomplish feats onstage that other tenors can only fantasize about. In the 1966 New York City Opera production of *La Traviata*, in the third act, Domingo was to carry soprano Patricia Brooks to the sofa where they would sing the "Parigi, o cara" duet. Domingo arrived late for the rehearsal and so began to sing while he was carrying her. It was so dramatically effective that director Frank Corsaro asked him to do it at the performance. Not many tenors have the physical strength, height, and breath control to accomplish this kind of feat. In a review of one of the *La Traviata* performances, the then chief music critic for the *New York Times*, Harold C. Schonberg, referred to Domingo as a "stentorian tenor who looked as if he could pick up the Empire State Building."

Rather than having his energy depleted by all of this activity, Domingo seems energized by it. In the 1982 *Opera News* article "What Makes Plácido Run," by Robert Jacobson, Domingo's friend Franco Iglesias described the power that the theater holds for Domingo: "...In his dressing room he prays and then goes to the stage, and when the curtain opens it's like he gets a shot of something. He sees the lights and the public and hears the music, and he is a completely different person." Of course, on his way to the stage he, like Pavarotti, must find a bent nail to bring him good luck.

In considering most things that are basically physical, the psychological element is not to be discounted. Domingo speaks passionately of his love for music and singing, and one can sense the energy that he generates.

Both singing and conducting require great physical, mental, and emotional effort, but Domingo has the rare ability to do both activities in the same day. He has been known to sing in an afternoon performance of *Parsifal*, Wagner's monumental work, which is also one of the most technically difficult to perform, then to go on—that evening—to conduct the three hours of Puccini's *Madama Butterfly*. He has also sung in a dress rehearsal of *Aïda* early in the day, conducted a staging rehearsal of *Carmen*

Above: Domingo sings the "Brindisi," or drinking song, in Act I of Verdi's **La Traviata** *at the Metropolitan Opera, 1981.*

a few hours later, then done the seemingly physically impossible: sung in a recording session (for the album *Unknown Puccini*) for five or six hours that night. With a schedule like this, Domingo is lucky that he is such a fast study; his ability to quickly absorb the most complicated musical and staging maneuvers is well-known and envied by fellow singers.

One wonders about so frenetic a schedule, and if Domingo is perhaps neurotically driven to maintain it. Perhaps he is trying to prove something. In a May 1995 *New York* magazine interview with David Daniel, Domingo provided an answer. "I've often thought that if I had not become a singer, I might have become a soccer player. It's just possible that deep inside of me I also want to test both my physical stamina and my ability to concentrate."

Not content with having multiple musical identities, Domingo has even found a way to juggle some of them simultaneously. In 1986, Domingo conducted Johann Strauss' *Die Fledermaus* for an Angel-EMI recording. Because of a last-minute casting problem, he was called upon to sing the role of Alfred and the track was mixed in.

More than one would expect from such a dynamo, there is an unassuming peacefulness about Domingo—

*Above: Domingo as **Parsifal** in the final scene of Wagner's final work, at the Metropolitan Opera. The great **Parsifal** is best described in Wagner's terms, as "a sacred festival drama," based on the Christian legend of the Holy Grail.*

saw his parents leave for a tour of Mexico, Cuba, and Puerto Rico. They had great success in Mexico and decided not to return to Spain, taking two years to get settled before sending for Plácido and his sister. The young boy was left with his aunt during their absence. He did finally join his parents, but it would be seventeen years before Plácido would see his native country again.

Plácido, of course, spent a great deal of time in the world of theater and zarzuela. At the age of nine, he won a children's competition for singing and dancing and began to take part in zarzuela performances with his parents. When Domingo was in his early teens, a young singer was needed in a production, and one of his contemporaries shoved him to the front of the stage. In his then baritone voice, the young Plácido shocked his father with his beautiful delivery. Domingo was technically a baritone. However, baritone roles in zarzuela lie fairly high in the voice. He was not reaching quite as high into the tenor territory as he soon would, but he was entering it substantially. It was as a baritone that he was to sing in zarzuelas and, at sixteen, in musicals such as *My Fair Lady* (in which he played one of the drunkards for 165 performances and also served as an assistant conductor and assistant coach). In early but true Domingo style, he and the company gave eight performances a week (every day, twice on Sunday).

It is typical of Domingo that he has never forgotten his roots, and he stays close to his extended family. He continues to return every year to the Teatro de la Zarzuela in Madrid, where his parents sang. He has also recorded zarzuelas, and his first season at Kennedy Center was constructed to include the zarzuela *El Gato Montes* ("The Wildcat") by Manuel Penella, which is about a bullfighter.

The life of a musician was not Domingo's first choice. As a boy in Spain, it is probably a rite of passage to want to become a bullfighter, and at age fourteen, Domingo tried his hand at the matador's art. This was in a special small ring where the courage of the young bulls, more than that of the young boys, was tested. Plácido's bull eventually must have made it into the big time, for the young Domingo quickly decided against bullfighting as a profession.

The life of a singer was not Domingo's parents' first choice for him, either. They felt that becoming a pianist (for which he also had great ability) would be more secure. They gave him piano lessons beginning at age eight, and

including a surprisingly quiet speaking voice—that contrasts with his rather frenetic image. The fact that his name means "Peaceful Sunday" has been said to be ironic, but this is a part of his nature, too. He probably would have been unable to sustain such activity if intensity were his only characteristic.

While Domingo may have inherited his passion for a life in music from his parents, he may have paid a price for it. His early life seems to have been a mix of the warmth and love of a close family life with the pain that a child faces when that life is interrupted. In Madrid, both of Domingo's parents were prominent performers of zarzuela, a quintessentially Spanish art form that dates back some three hundred years. Zarzuela is closely related in form and feeling to operetta and, in some respects, to the American musical. His mother, Pepita Embil, was given the title "The Queen of Zarzuela," and composers wrote works specifically for her voice. His father, Plácido Domingo, Sr., though he damaged his voice by singing with a cold, was able to continue in zarzuela because of its substantial spoken dialogue. At the age of six, Domingo

he went on to study theory, history, and basic conducting, in addition to voice. This well-rounded, complete musical education served him well. Placido first conducted at the age of sixteen, in the classic zarzuela *Luisa Fernanda*, with both of his parents in the cast.

Singing and studying did not occupy all of young Plácido's time. He fell in love with a fellow student and eloped. Although the marriage did not last more than a year, it produced a son (whose daughter's birth would make Domingo a grandfather by age forty). It also produced the need to earn a living, which the naturally versatile Domingo solved by playing piano for strippers in a nightclub. It was not too long after the end of his first marriage that Domingo met and married Marta Ornelas (a native of Mexico City), the woman who has been his wife and partner since.

The word *"partner"* is particularly apt for Marta, who was one of the top singers at the Mexico Opera. They had known each other since their conservatory days. It was Marta who first detected a flaw in her new husband's breathing technique and worked with him to overcome it. They were very much a team, personally and professionally, in Mexico City and then in Israel, until they were expecting their first child. At that point, Marta decided to devote her time to their family and not to singing. Domingo's personal and professional closeness to his wife, however, has not prevented the rumor mill from churning out stories of his romantic liaisons, linking him with royalty, members of society, and other celebrities (including actresses Gina Lollobrigida and Susan Anton).

Plácido Domingo's career began in earnest—and defined who he was as an artist—in 1959, when he auditioned for the Mexico National Opera as a baritone. The perceptive auditioners realized that the natural tessitura of his voice was higher than he realized, and they engaged him as a tenor. He made his operatic debut in *La Traviata* and, also that year, sang in the Dallas Civic Opera's *Lucia di Lammermoor* with Joan Sutherland.

In 1962, Domingo and Marta (who had been married that year) accepted an offer from the Israel National Opera (also called the Hebrew National Opera) to go to Tel Aviv for a six-month stint as the leading tenor and soprano. They stayed two and a half years, with Domingo singing approximately three hundred performances in

Above: **In the 1986 television special "Plácido Domingo Sings Zarzuela!"** *the tenor sings a duet with Josefina Arregui, a member of the* **Antología de la Zarzuela** *touring company.*

Above: Plácido Domingo and his wife, Marta, were married in 1962.

twelve operas. And because of the international makeup of the country, Domingo was able to extend his knowledge of languages. He speaks four—English, French, Italian, and his native Spanish—but sings in even more, including, of course, Hebrew.

In *My First Forty Years*, Domingo wrote extensively about their time in Israel. "The company was extraordinary. Franco [Iglesias, a baritone who was a good friend of the Domingos] once had to cancel an appearance in *La Traviata*, and the baritone who replaced him had not sung the part of Germont in Italian for a long time. He sang in Hungarian; the soprano knew the part of Violetta only in German; I did Alfredo in Italian; and the chorus performed in Hebrew. Fortunately, the conductor was

leading in Esperanto. We had a United Nations cast for *Don Giovanni*, too: the conductor, Arthur Hammond, was British; two Mexicans, Marta and Franco, sang Donna Elvira and Masetto; a Spaniard, myself, was Don Ottavio; Michiko Sunahara was our Japanese Zerlina; Donna Anna was Greek—Athena Lampropoulos; Don Giovanni, Livio Pombeni, was Italian; and William Valentine, a black bass from Mississippi, sang Leporello. Such casting was considered absolutely normal."

Domingo's time in Israel was a period of discovery—of music, of the world, and how he fit into both. It was also a time of experimentation, and points to how important it is for an artist to be able to take chances, to see what works and what does not, and to adjust accordingly. Away from the major stages of the world capitals, yet being among fine performers and demanding audiences, Domingo had the opportunity to find his voice in more ways than one.

Perhaps most importantly, Domingo was able to develop a breathing technique that would allow him to produce not only a beautiful, controlled sound but also to increase the longevity of his career. In his 1972 *New York Times* article "The More I Sing the Better I Sound," Gerald Walker described the development of Domingo's breath control: "Domingo was at the end of his first year in Tel Aviv before he heard about this basic singing technique....Domingo was doing the chest-out-stomach-in 'high breathing' he had learned in gym class. Self-taught as a singer...he had his vocal method diaphragm backwards. 'Before you take a high note,' Iglesias explained, 'the diaphragm should not go up but all the way down and the stomach out, providing room for the lungs to expand and fill with breath. The down-thrust diaphragm and out-thrust abdomen provide enough pressure on the column of air being forced up between the vocal cords to make them vibrate strongly and produce more sound.'"

In 1968, Domingo made his Metropolitan Opera debut in the kind of emergency situation that a day later makes it newsworthy and years later makes it legendary. Such a debut, on a half hour's notice, can finish off lesser talents than Domingo's. A call from the late Rudolf Bing (general manager of the Metropolitan Opera from 1950 to 1972) had Domingo on the great stage as a substitute for Franco Corelli in the role of Maurizio in *Adriana Lecouvreur*. Marta was too pregnant to make the last-minute drive into the city from their home in New Jersey, leaving Plácido's father as the sole means of emotional support—and the driver. As they made their way south on the West Side Highway, Domingo began to vocalize, warming up the voice for the big moment. Coming to a temporary stop, Domingo saw the people in the next car laughing at him. According to his autobiography, in true New York style, he rolled down the window and asked where they were going. They were headed to the Met. "Well, don't laugh," he told them, "because you'll be hearing me in a few minutes!" Domingo later admitted that with more advance notice he probably would have been far more nervous.

Above: Plácido Domingo in the title role of Mozart's comic opera Idomeneo, *Metropolitan Opera, 1994.*

Above: Plácido Domingo rehearses the title role in Verdi's Otello *in New York with Gilda Cruz-Romo as Desdemona. This was for the opening of the 1979 Metropolitan Opera season.*

Since then, Domingo has been relentless in his desire to sing often and well. But even with all of his great success, he remains easy to work with, a colleague who does not pull rank or indulge in egocentric demonstrations. He is known to be cooperative and generous. The good of the performance is Domingo's main concern. There is temperament—without that there would be no color or emotional edge to the performance—but not temperamentality. He is also described as dependable, not a great word in the performing arts as it can be misunderstood to mean dull. In Domingo's case, it refers to the fact that he rarely cancels performances, always knows his part thoroughly, and delivers performances that usually range from very good to thrilling.

Domingo earns high praise from his fellow artists, further testament to the fact that the esteem in which he is held worldwide is not simply a result of expert marketing but is truly deserved. Annalyn Swan and Abigail Kuflik, in *Newsweek* magazine, neatly summed up Domingo's colleagues' opinions of him: "Conductors speak of his superb musical instincts, directors of how cooperative he is, singers of his teamwork—soprano Teresa Stratas calls him a 'dream partner'—and stage-hands about what a nice guy he is. To top it off, his modesty, in a world of swollen egos, is staggering." Unlike some of his fellow opera stars, Domingo does not seem to possess an ego that prevents him from performing simple, frequent acts of kindness for those close to him as well as for those he does not know. In Israel, on the days of Marta's performances, he would cook for her; on his performance days, she cooked for him.

The late soprano Patricia Brooks, who was swept off her feet by Domingo in *La Traviata*, noted Domingo's extraordinary generosity toward her in those performances. In *I Remember Too Much* by Dennis McGovern and Deborah Grace Winer, Brooks recalled, "In the farewell to Alfredo, Placido used to give me singing lessons. He'd turn his back to the audience and show me how to place it [the production of her voice]. He's such a sweetheart—there are very few tenors who would do that."

Below: Teresa Stratas and Plácido Domingo share a tender moment in **La Traviata.**

Above: At the rehearsal for the Metropolitan Opera's 1984 Spring Gala (front row, left to right) the late John Denver, Plácido Domingo, the late Yves Montand, and Lionel Richie. This was the final event of the Met's Centennial season celebrations.

missions. Then in October, Domingo asked to be released from all commitments for a year to perform in major fund-raising benefits for the earthquake victims.

Domingo has been known to sing an entire aria spontaneously for a delighted fan who was not able to obtain a ticket to the performance. Even in his book, *My First Forty Years*, he was kind to his colleagues. Some of the book's critics, in fact, accused him of being too nice, not sharing backstage tales that would make colleagues look bad. Domingo admitted that if he does not have something good to say, he does not say it.

In the 1982 *New York* magazine article by Peter G. Davis "Pop Goes Domingo," the tenor gave his philosophy of performing: "I would like to be remembered as someone who brought three things to his performing: honesty, excitement, and peace. First, I must serve composers, because without them we singers are nothing. Then, like every performer, I must excite the public, but I also hope people will find peace in my singing and perhaps forget their

Domingo's generosity is not limited to his fellow cast members. His relatives are frequent recipients of great thoughtfulness, for family milestones (which he always remembers), and in times of tragedy. In September 1985, devastating earthquakes hit Mexico. With four of his family members missing (an aunt, uncle, cousin, and the cousin's small child), Domingo opened the Chicago Lyric Opera's season, then flew directly to Mexico City, canceling other performances to help dig through the rubble to search for them. All four had been killed in the collapse of their apartment building, but Domingo stayed on to work even after their bodies had been found. He used his celebrity standing to make public pleas for additional heavy equipment, supplies, and volunteers for rescue

problems for a while." A year later, Domingo went further. "I feel very deeply," he told John Gruen in a 1983 article in *Pan Am Clipper* magazine, "that with music you can do much good in the world....You can unite people through music. When audiences sit listening to music, they seem truly at peace with themselves—it's like a communion."

Domingo is a beloved artist, but no one of his stature is able to remain free of all criticism. If there is one complaint that is heard at all—albeit not loudly or frequently— it is that Domingo's performances do not always have great intensity of feeling, do not always give the listener or operagoer that rare feeling of danger, of being on the edge of some incredible adventure or of the unknown. Some feel that the price Domingo pays for being an untemperamental, dependable artist is that his perfor-mances, while passionate and convincing, are not at that exalted level that makes them unforgettable.

As with any great singer, Domingo's sound is uniquely his. It is the way he colors his voice that allows him to communicate the more subtle aspects of the characters he portrays. His vocal color can change from phrase to phrase, word to word.

Domingo offered an insight into this process in a 1971 article by Alan Blythe in the magazine *Gramophone*. When asked about singing Otello, Placido commented that "...I must wait until I've understood every aspect of the part, so that I can color the phrases as they should be colored. You know there is much more to it than just heroics."

So what will happen to this human dynamo when nature reclaims the gift of his voice? The last subject most singers want to think about is the eventual, inevitable loss of the voice. This is not so much an abrupt loss as a deterioration. Pitch will no longer be exact, tone no longer clear and beautiful, and the highest notes no longer reachable.

But Domingo is an exception. He freely discusses his postperformance plans, to which he has obviously given great thought. He is very well prepared it seems, psychologically and practically. With the Washington Opera and Los Angeles Music Center Opera administrative positions in place, and with his substantial and still-growing number of conducting engagements, Domingo has given himself exceptional options. He has also expressed an interest in having a full-time music directorship, a school for young singers, and a record label to direct, thus letting it be known that such invitations would be considered. One dream that will not have to wait is his desire to be a restauranteur: Domingo, the restau-rant, opened on Manhattan's 49th Street in 1996.

When—and if—his voice finally goes, Domingo might find himself truly liberated as a conductor. The art of conducting is elusive and mysterious. The conductor him-self does not create the sound but influences it. He or she must know the score totally—every note played by every instrumentalist; the character of each instrument's sound, and how each should blend as part of the whole; the over-all architecture of the work (how it should develop, what should be stressed, when and how it should build to smaller and larger climaxes); the character of individual phrases (which will determine the personality of the total work); and the general concept of the work philo-sophically. All of this must begin with instinct but be shaped by study—of the basic theory of music as well as its history and tradition, and the history and traditions of the various cultures that have influenced the music's creation and re-creation.

Below: Josefina Howard and Plácido and Marta Domingo at the opening of his New York City restaurant, Domingo, in 1996.

At the moment, many believe that Domingo is not a conductor of great complexity or subtlety; some even say that if he were not already famous he would not be given the prominent podiums on which he is conducting. This is not a completely fair judgement. Most conductors start when they are very young and develop on the smaller podiums of the world, learning on the job in front of the less-important critics and other professionals. Domingo did not have this opportunity, and it is possible that, as he gains experience, his ability will grow proportionately. One must remember that while Domingo does not consider himself a natural tenor, he does consider himself to be a natural conductor. In a 1985 article in *Ovation* magazine, Domingo was open about this: "I'm not a born tenor," he said. "It was really a fight for me to get the high notes. I am not one of those singers who opened his mouth and found a high C right away. But," he added, "I think I have the feeling of being a born conductor." One can look forward to what he will try to accomplish.

Throughout his life, no matter what he has done—conduct or sing—Domingo has been blessed by both talent and luck. And he helps his luck along, not only by finding and pocketing preperformance bent nails, but with a post-opera ritual: after the last performance in a series, he returns to the stage, now only a shadowy, silent witness to the performance that occurred not long before. Here, Domingo says "au revoir" to the stage and the theater, to ensure that he will, indeed, return. For all these years, the gods must have been listening.

Left: It is not unusual for Plácido Domingo to receive flowers and long ovations after his performances, all over the world. He seems to welcome the displays of affection from his public, and has been known to serenade a single fan backstage who was not able to obtain a ticket to the performance.

Above: Plácido Domingo belts out his part at the Three Tenors concert at Wembly.

José Carreras

WHEN JOSÉ CARRERAS WALKED ONTO THE CARACALLA STAGE AT THE *THREE TENORS* CONCERT IN 1990, THE OVATION HE RECEIVED WAS FOR MORE THAN "JUST" BEING ONE OF THE WORLD'S BEST-KNOWN SINGERS. IT WAS FOR BEING A HERO OF SORTS: CARRERAS HAD ONLY RECENTLY WON A MAJOR ROUND IN HIS FIGHT AGAINST A RARE AND DEADLY FORM OF LEUKEMIA AFTER ENDURING A FRIGHTFUL YEAR OF TORTUROUS TREATMENT.

Above: José Carreras in Seattle, 1990, at his first solo recital in the
United States following his recovery from leukemia.
Previous page: With boyish good looks and the real-life story of a hero,
José Carreras has won the devotion of opera lovers for his talent, and their
admiration for surviving, with grace, a nearly fatal disease.

Carreras was born in Barcelona in 1946. As with Pavarotti and Domingo, the love of singing, if not of music itself, had been part of his life since childhood. But unlike the other two, no one in the Carreras family had any interest in music. His father was a teacher who, after fighting on the Republican side in the Spanish Civil War, was not permitted by Franco's forces to return to his profession as a teacher; instead, he worked as a member of the traffic police. His mother was a hairdresser. So he did not have the advantage of early exposure to the art.

Carreras's initial musical inspiration came from the big screen when, at the age of seven, he saw Mario Lanza in *The Great Caruso*. Carreras said that he has not stopped singing since then. In a 1993 *UNESCO Courier* interview, Carreras recalled the impact Lanza's singing had on him: "The day after I saw the film I started imitating Mario Lanza, and I noticed I was able to reproduce almost all the arias in *The Great Caruso*, which I'd never heard before, with startling accuracy. My parents weren't exactly great opera-lovers, but they were so impressed, they started wondering whether my love of music was not after all a sign that I really had a vocation. They gave me a record-player and records of *The Great Caruso* and Neapolitan songs sung by Giuseppe Di Stefano. I was absolutely thrilled. I was eight when my father enrolled me at the Barcelona Conservatory and took me for the first time to a performance of Verdi's *Aïda* at the Liceo [the Gran Teatre del Liceu, also known as the Teatro Liceo] in Barcelona. It was pure magic! Attending a live performance of an opera, with all the singers, the orchestra, the sets, the atmosphere and all the rest, was a decisive experience for me."

Just before his trip to the opera house, José had made his first public appearance as a singer, on a radio program fund raiser to benefit needy children. He sang a Catalan Christmas song and the aria "La donna è mobile"

Right: José Carreras in **Jerusalem**, Vienna 1995.

Above: Carreras with fellow Spaniard, soprano Montserrat Caballé, who sang the title role in Cilea's Adriana Lecouvreur *to Carreras' Maurizio, at the Metropolitan Opera, 1978.*

from *Rigoletto*. His talents were impressive enough to earn him an invitation to sing in a production of the opera *Retablo de Maese Pedro*, by Manuel de Falla, one of Spain's greatest composers, at the Liceo itself. In a boyishly high voice, Carreras performed on that legendary stage, singing a difficult part originally written for soprano. His parents realized that their son had exceptional talent and began to think about steering him toward a professional career. But their enthusiasm was properly tempered by the celebrated Spanish pianist and conductor José Iturbi, who made them aware that the critical test—puberty and the changing of their son's voice—was yet to come.

In coming years, José, aware of the uncertainties of the music business, added science and chemistry to his music studies. But like many boys growing up in Spain, he flirted with the idea of a career in sports, particularly soccer. Many years later, it would be a passion for that sport that would figure significantly in bringing together The Three Tenors. But it was not until he was twenty-one that Carreras decided to embrace singing as his life's work.

His first major break came in 1970, when he was twenty-four years old. He sang the minor role of Flavio in Bellini's *Norma* with the Spanish soprano Montserrat Caballé singing the title role, and less than a year later, she invited him to sing the male lead opposite her in Donizetti's *Lucrezia Borgia* at the Liceo. Carreras considers his performance in *Lucrezia Borgia* his real debut.

In the world of professional opera, everyone knows everyone else, and the debut, or first major performance, of an especially promising young artist is anticipated, observed, dissected, and analyzed—sometimes with delight at the discovery of major new talent, sometimes with badly concealed resentment if it is someone else's student or someone else's client. But success is always noted, and a career can be given an important boost from a successful performance in a major venue, as it was for Carreras in 1970.

In 1971, Carreras decided to enter the Verdi Singing Competition in Parma, Italy, in spite of the fact that he had not been successful at a competition in Barcelona three years earlier. There are certain types of musicians who do the "competition circuit" very well, and others whose personalities are not suited to that kind of intense pressure and blatant comparison to other musicians. Carreras had his doubts but felt that, at worst, he would gain additional performing experience. But he won, receiving money and a Parma opera house debut as part of the prize. After his successful appearance, Carreras was invited back the following season, and another major step in building his career had been taken. One of the unofficial "prizes" from the Parma competition was an introduction to the tenor Giuseppe Di Stefano, one of his childhood heroes who had become a professional role model and whom the young Carreras was said to have resembled vocally. They became good friends, with the elder tenor giving the newcomer valuable advice and support.

Other opera house debuts came within the next few years: the New York City Opera in 1972, with the Vienna Staatsoper, Munich National Theatre, London Royal Opera House, La Scala, and the Metropolitan Opera following in quick succession. Caballé was not the only important musician to champion the young Carreras. The La Scala debut brought him to the attention of the eminent conductor Herbert von Karajan, and Carreras was invited by von Karajan to sing in Verdi's *Requiem* in Salzburg during the Easter Festival, an impressive and important musical engagement that was another important step in Carreras' career. The first rehearsal, however, provided the young singer with one of his worst professional moments: his voice simply stopped working. When he

Above: A young Carreras, twenty-seven years old, in 1973, only one year before his first major career break: singing opposite Montserrat Caballé in Lucrezia Borgia, *which he considers to have been his real debut.*

Above: Carreras as Riccardo (Gustavus) in Verdi's Un Ballo in maschera, *at the San Francisco Opera, 1977.*

Carreras had been a successful musician long before his bout with cancer, deservedly earning a reputation as one of the world's top tenors. He was not considered on a par with Pavarotti and Domingo, but on the level just below: not one of the top two tenors, but one of the top three. And so there is some irony in the fact that without Carreras, the Three Tenors phenomenon probably would not have happened. Domingo and Pavarotti agreed to perform in the 1990 Rome concert mainly to celebrate Carreras' return to life and to opera. Without such a reason to convene, the event might not have taken place at all; it certainly would not have had the joyous spirit that became its hallmark.

By the mid-1980s, Carreras had begun to have vocal problems. At such a relatively young age (he was in his late thirties), singers facing vocal problems have usually overextended themselves, giving in to the temptation of accepting too many dates and pushing the voice into singing roles for which it is basically not suited. Such was the case with Carreras. His voice began to show evidence of wear and tear, losing some of its great facility and its tonal clarity, particularly in the high notes. The early days of Carreras' career held the promise of true musical greatness and longevity. A *New York Times* review by Harold C. Schonberg in 1974 underscored this great potential: "In short, he is a prize, and is by far the best tenor the City Opera has had since the young Plácido Domingo." But that promise was never fully realized. Past a certain point of abuse, the delicate vocal equipment will not fully recover.

Young singers are frequently pushed into performing too much, too soon. Talent today is rarely allowed to develop slowly and naturally; young musicians are often urged to perform as much as possible as soon as possible. Singers must have time to grow into roles, especially the heavier ones, naturally. Like an athlete, a musician needs to be focused emotionally and in good shape physically. While a tired instrumentalist does have to deal with a weakened body, his instrument can still be in optimum shape. A tired or ill singer risks everything when he opens his mouth.

It is easy to give in to the temptation to overbook oneself, but the ability to do so much professionally is a rather recent development. Major changes in the music profession occurred in the late 1950s and early 1960s

opened his mouth, no sounds were produced. He was a scant yard away from von Karajan, an intimidating giant of a musician, and he simply could not sing. But Carreras recovered for the performances, and von Karajan recognized him as a young singer with musical qualities that were not only outstanding, but very much in sympathy with his own. They were to work together many times before von Karajan's death in 1989, with Carreras enjoying what he called "the most extraordinary and important relationship in my artistic life."

Like his countryman Domingo, Carreras has a clear, rich voice with the somewhat "darker" sound characteristic of Spanish singers. Both men's voices are often described as honeyed, sensual, and velvety; the word "ringing" is seldom used with voices such as theirs. But unlike Domingo, Carreras has always been a pure lyric tenor, without dips into the upper range of the baritone register. Although Carreras' voice is now darkening as he is getting older, he will probably never successfully cross the border into true dramatic repertory. It is simply not for his quality voice.

Above: Carreras at the Metropolitan Opera in Bizet's Carmen, *with the American soprano Leona Mitchell, 1987.*

when jet travel became commonplace, allowing musicians to shuttle all over the world, all the time. Before then, they could travel only by ship and train. Not only was there enforced leisure en route, with time for artists to rest, think, and communicate, but even more importantly, they were unable to sing or play more than a limited number of performances within a given time. One could not, as is done today, give a concert in New York, fly to Paris late that night or early the next morning, have a rehearsal the next day, fly to another European city for another rehearsal two days after that, then race back to Paris for a performance—often of completely different repertory in each city. At about the same time that jet planes began shuttling musicians around the globe, concert halls and opera houses were sprouting up throughout the United States. So there were a lot more performances to be given. But this did not mean that a great many more musicians would be employed. It meant that many of the same ones—the more famous, of course—would perform more dates, appearing in more cities, more often.

While the brunt of the blame for overextending himself was placed on Carreras, part of it was given to his mentor, Herbert von Karajan, who, some say, had pushed Carreras into roles that were too heavy for him. The result, as described by the *New York Times'* John Rockwell (in a May, 1989 review where he wrote about Carreras' past vocal problems) was "a darkening of timbre and a loss of ease on top, coupled with a sometimes overly emphatic delivery that coarsened both his voice and the musical line." Will Crutchfield, then a *New York Times* music critic, reviewed a performance of Carreras singing a zarzuela program in Avery Fisher Hall in 1986. He raised serious questions about the quality of Carreras' voice, asking, "Why not, then, quit complaining and simply enjoy him for what he is? Because we cannot forget what he was. If an unknown tenor appeared tomorrow singing exactly as Mr. Carreras sang Sunday, we would welcome him as a solid, presentable singer with some trouble on the top, but we would not say that here was something special, something potentially wonderful—and that is what people did say, with reason, when Mr. Carreras appeared on the scene about a dozen years ago."

Carreras admitted to giving in to the temptation of singing too much in a 1989 interview with Allan Kozinn,

Left: Carreras sings at an informal rehearsal.

also of the *New York Times*: "I made some mistakes, as everyone does. Perhaps I agreed to do certain things when I knew they would be too much. But it is hard for someone with a real vocation for opera to say no. When you have 365 offers a year, from conductors like Claudio Abbado, Riccardo Muti, Herbert von Karajan, and James Levine, and you agree to do 80 of those performances, you are already saying no almost 300 times."

Ironically, it was the great tragedy of Carreras' life that gave him back some of the transparency and purity of tonal quality he had before the mid-1980s. In the autumn of 1987, after a somewhat less hectic summer than usual, Carreras began filming *La Bohème* in Paris. Soon after the filming began, Carreras developed an infection in a newly implanted tooth. Despite a round of antibiotics, the infection persisted and Carreras felt increasingly run down. It was this seemingly minor problem that revealed an abnormality in his blood count. At the age of forty-one, the singer was diagnosed with acute lymphocytic leukemia. At the time of diagnosis, he was not far from death. In any profession, reports of ill health can be damaging; for a performer, they can be disastrous. Most opera companies book artists two seasons in advance, so reports of a health problem often send executive directors scurrying in another artist's direction, leaving the singer basically without bookings two seasons hence. Opera directors want to avoid problems whenever possible, and so will avoid hiring an artist who might, from ill health, turn in a poor-quality performance, or who might have an increased chance of cancellation.

A *New York Times* article in August 1987 stated: "Reports in the European press that José Carreras has cancer were denied yesterday by the Spanish tenor's New York management....The forty-one-year-old singer had been hospitalized in Paris for a 'toxicity in his blood system.' The condition, which has occurred several times in the last year, is the result of dental problems and an adverse reaction to antibiotics...." So, while dealing with horrendous medical procedures, Carreras and his family had to work at keeping the press at bay—including photographers who dressed in medical staff gowns in attempts to invade his room. Newspapers readied his obituaries for publication, recording companies prepared memorial recordings for release, and other artists dedicated performances to him—some complete with moments of silence.

Above: Carreras sings the role of Don José in a 1990 production of **Carmen** *in Vienna.*

Above: Carreras in La Bohème, *1982, at the Metropolitan Opera, with soprano Teresa Stratas. This Puccini opera has a tragic ending, but provides moments of lightness and sweetness, as well as some of the most memorable melodies ever written.*

Carreras' treatment regimen began with chemotherapy but was not limited to that; chemotherapy would allow only for the possibility of remission, but would not be enough to cure the disease. The chance of a complete cure could come only from a bone marrow transplant. With time running out and a suitable donor having not been found (including among members of Carreras' own family), it was decided that the best course would be to remove his own bone marrow, which would be treated, cleansed of cancer cells, and restored to his body. Surviving this treatment, with its pain and risk but with no guarantee of success, would be a torturous process, physically and emotionally. After undergoing three rounds of chemotherapy in Barcelona, Carreras was transferred to the renowned

Fred Hutchinson Cancer Research Center in Seattle for the actual transplant, a process that would last eight weeks.

To start, more than a quart of his own marrow was extracted from several hundred punctures in his pelvis. The marrow would be cleansed of cancer cells, then frozen, until Carreras' body had been prepared to properly receive it. Soon after the marrow was withdrawn, more chemotherapy was given. And to be sure that every cancer cell in his body had been destroyed, full-bolt radiation treatments were also administered, in three twenty-minute sessions a day for five days. Again, not only was the treatment itself dreadful, but its painful effects lasted for weeks. He endured constant nausea, a fungal infection in the mouth and throat, and a central vein catheter that remained in his body (through which he received medication and nutrition, and through which six blood samples a day were taken) for six months. He was not able to swallow for months.

Once the two-week danger period after the transplant had passed and Carreras seemed to be doing well, he thought the worst was behind him. But the new marrow had become "paralyzed," as Carreras describes it, and a full-scale crisis developed. A new drug, GMCSF, was administered, and the marrow was reactivated.

During the seemingly interminable radiation treatments he received, Carreras tried to escape his

surroundings through music, and was able to judge how much time had elapsed by singing works whose timings he knew. As he wrote in his book, *José Carreras Singing from the Soul*, "I felt so miserable, so weak, that I tried to forget where I was. To pass the time, I began to sing, very softly, songs and arias. I knew just how long they were, from the timings of my recordings, and so I knew how much time was passing and how soon it would be over." The chemicals filled his body, but the music filled his mind. With the powerful connection between mind and body, it is possible that both were powerful healing forces. By the time the radiation treatments had ended, Carreras had lost forty

Below: Home in Barcelona in 1988, Carreras holds a press conference about his bone marrow transplant for leukemia at the Fred Hutchinson Cancer Research Center in Seattle.

Above: Carreras returning to good health, to the concert stage, and to Barcelona, in 1988, after his year-long illness and absence from the stage.

Carreras' body through a device which had been installed in a vein in his shoulder. It was hoped that the now-healthy bone marrow cells, traveling through the bloodstream, would find their way into his bones and reproduce, slowly restoring him to a state of good health. Carreras was aware that his chances of survival were slim; his type of leukemia kills nine out of ten of its victims within five years. He was also aware of what the illness and the treatments could do to his voice: his vocal cords could have been harmed, or the mucus membranes dried out by radiation. In his worst moments, he was unable even to speak. Out of fear that breathing tubes would damage his vocal cords, Carreras endured medical procedures without general anesthesia.

It may be difficult for nonmusicians to fully understand what music means to those who have devoted their lives to it. It goes far beyond the enjoyment of specific works or the interpretations of certain performers. Far stronger than that, it often involves a spirituality that approaches religious feeling, deeply affecting one emotionally and offering a philosophy

pounds and, because he was constantly in danger of falling prey to other infections, had to be isolated from family and friends. This was especially difficult for a man who loves being with people. (Even at the opera house just before a performance, when many artists seek seclusion, Carreras will arrive at the theater long before the starting time and, as he wrote in his autobiography "...I welcome the distraction when friends and colleagues drop by my dressing room to chat for a moment.") Such isolation intensified the horror of what he was experiencing.

When the chemotherapy and radiation treatments were complete, the cleansed marrow was put back into

of connectedness not just to art and artists but to one's inner self and to one's fellow beings on the most universal level. Carreras' doctor asked him not to put his singing voice to a test, but he disobeyed, quietly starting to sing in the bath. In *The New York Times* article "José Carreras Begins a European Tour," in December 1988, Carreras explained, "If you are burned, you are naturally anxious to see what your face looks like as soon as they take the bandages off. In my case, it was my voice that was my main concern." As with most people in crisis, Carreras was not above asking a dangerous—and unanswerable—question. In the same *New York Times* article, he said, "My first reaction was to ask over and over, 'Why me?' But when I was moved to the hospital, my floor had twelve rooms, and in eight of those the leukemia patients were little children. Then you don't ask, 'Why me?' anymore."

If the downside of being a celebrity is having the paparazzi ever present, the upside is receiving, as did Carreras, more than 150,000 pieces of mail from admirers sending love and concern, good thoughts, and prayers for recovery. This was yet another psychological element that Carreras feels directly benefited his physical condition.

The Fred Hutchinson Cancer Research Center was Carreras' home from November 1987 to March 1988. He left there not knowing if his treatment had been effective but with the reassurance that he had had the finest care available. As a gesture of gratitude, one of his first major appearances after his illness was a benefit for "The Hutch," as the center is affectionately known. But the real debut of the new Carreras voice, his first concert after his bout with leukemia, took place at Barcelona's Arch of Triumph (the city's main park) in July 1988, before an audience of 150,000, which included Spain's Queen Sofia. There was no admission fee, but contributions were accepted for Carreras' new foundation, The José Carreras International Leukemia Foundation, established to fight leukemia. Carreras referred to the concert as his second debut, and understandably called the event "the most incredible, the most touching moment of my life."

A second concert, also to benefit his foundation, took place the following month at the Arena in Verona. Most relapses of Carreras' type of illness occur within one year. Within that year, not only was Carreras well, he was singing again. But how was he singing? The reviews were almost unanimous in saying that his voice was not only

still very much "there" but seemed to be of even better quality than before. The enforced rest had had a healing effect on his voice, reversing some of the damage caused by abuse and overuse.

In *Newsday* on May 27, 1989, Peter Goodman reviewed Carreras' return to Carnegie Hall: "...By the end of the first set—songs by Scarlatti, Bellini and Stradella—it was apparent that Carreras' voice had not suffered from his illness....By the end of the evening it was obvious that Carreras is once again a member of that select threesome, rejoining Luciano Pavarotti and Plácido Domingo as the premier tenors in the world today. He sounded better Thursday night than he had in years, long preceding the cancer, when ambition and an often unwise choice of repertory had worn and tugged his voice ragged. Pavarotti has the clarion brilliance and almost puppyish charm;

Above: Carreras accepts a large donation for his Foundation at the HMV 75th Anniversary Charity Gala in London, February 1996.

Left: José Carreras performing an encore during his U.S. concert tour, 1993. Carreras is known for his intense and heartfelt interpretations of works ranging from operatic masterpieces to popular songs.

Domingo is darker in tone and more willing to struggle for meaning and emotion. But Carreras, who was always more sweetly lyrical, has a blend of passion and reserve that wins respect and admiration....The dignity and understated pride of Carreras' manner gave his interpretations an impact that went beyond superficial emotionalism.... There was an openness and ease in his voice that had been missing before, while the shy intensity of his performance was deeply affecting."

The New York Times' John Rockwell agreed: "...Mr. Carreras' voice still has a lot of honey left. Maybe even more than before his illness." That kind of comment, however, must be put into proper perspective: it did not mean that he was back to the voice of the young Carreras, before the vocal problems began, but that he was not worse off vocally than he was before his illness. Indeed, the enforced rest of the vocal cords may have had a beneficial effect on his voice. But it did not restore him to the time before he did too much, too soon. Bernard Holland, in a 1992 *New York Times* review of a Carreras concert at Carnegie Hall, referred to his situation: "The big serviceable, rough-edged delivery is intact, but there has been no retreat toward the golden sound that promised so much at the beginning of his career."

Of all the operatic characters he has portrayed, Carreras feels that the poet Rodolfo in *La Bohème* most closely resembles his own personality. Carreras is known as a good colleague, cooperative, kind, and relatively free of egocentric temperamentality.

And like his successful colleagues, Carreras has performed and recorded his share of pop music, for which he has expressed genuine appreciation. Before *The Three Tenors*, Carreras had become known to the general public not just through opera but through his recordings of *West Side Story* and *South Pacific*. His voice, beautifully scaled to the relative simplicity of pop tunes, seems better suited to this kind of music than the voices of many of his operatic

Right: Carreras with Greek mezzo-soprano Agnes Baltsa in the finale of Bizet's **Carmen**, *Vienna, 1990*.

brethren. In *José Carreras Singing from the Soul,* Carreras identified his reasons for singing popular music. "First, I enjoy it, as do millions of other fans. I also find it relaxing to sing. But deep down I confess to an ulterior motive: I sing popular tunes because I believe that this is the way to capture new fans for the opera. My hope is that record buyers who listen to *South Pacific* and *West Side Story* may develop an interest in Carreras the vocalist and then discover through him a whole new world of beauty and fascination—the opera."

Carreras' acting has always been marked by intensity, sincerity and directness. He also has the good looks of a movie star and an unusually appealing manner on stage. Slender in build, with a delicate handsomeness, Carreras seems to appeal to a younger female audience more than do his two tenor colleagues.

But offstage, in his own life, Carreras seems to appeal mightily to grown women. Like Pavarotti and Domingo, Carreras has had his share of reported liaisons, some while married to Mercedes Perez, whom he wed in 1971. With her, Carreras had two children, a son, Alberto, and a daughter, Julia. It was during an apparent eight-year relationship with Austrian airline stewardess Jutte Jaeger that Mercedes left José (in June 1992, after twenty-one years of marriage). Jutte was with José during his illness, but eventually married another man. The media grabs onto any opportunity it can, reporting any Carreras sighting that may involve romantic interest.

Although Carreras has been experiencing vocal problems for some time, he may still have years of singing ahead of him. But when he does retire from the stage, he has expressed a desire to devote himself full-time to his foundation. To date, his foundation has raised more than $10 million.

Since his rebirth in 1988 as a performing artist, Carreras has—to list just some of his activities—sung at Atlantic City's Taj Mahal casino (in a tribute to Mario

Above: José Carreras (second from left) and Zubin Mehta (second from right) arrive at the airport
in Sarajevo, 1994, for a televised benefit performance of Mozart's Requiem. The concert was held in
the burned-out ruins of the National Library, which had been ignited by a Serb shell in 1992.

Lanza); toured cities in North America; devoted time to his foundation (and has been on television in public service announcements for bone marrow donors); served as music director of the 1992 Summer Olympics' opening and closing ceremonies in Barcelona (singing in both events); given a well-received recital in Carnegie Hall in 1992; participated in a televised benefit performance of Mozart's *Requiem* in the bombed-out shell of Bosnia's National Library in Sarajevo; and, of course, made history as one of the Three Tenors.

Carreras is considered to have an inquiring intellectual mind with interests in politics (as an observer, not a potential candidate); poetry (reading it, not writing it); painting (appreciating the talents of the great painters, not trying his own hand at it).

From surviving a life-threatening disease, Carreras' sense of values has been considerably changed. "I realized," he wrote in *Singing from the Soul*, "how superficial and life-draining it was for someone to assert, 'Oh, I'd love to do this, but I'm afraid I don't have the time!' This kind of statement is nothing more than a vulgar lie. Can you conceive of anything more enriching than to accomplish what you've always wanted? And who's to say you don't have the time?"

His professional outlook has changed, too. "I don't need to kill myself working any more and I don't have to prove anything to anyone, absolutely nothing at all. And most importantly, there's nothing more I have to prove to myself for I am aware of what I can do and I know where I stand. What more do I want?"

The post-leukemia changes to Carreras also involved his approach to the music itself, with evidence of a new maturity, a new emotional depth, and a new appreciation of his art. "I no longer care who is number one or two or ten or sixty, or who is doing this premiere or that recording," Carreras told Nancy Malitz in a 1989 *Ovation* magazine article. "I will sing because it is a great privilege."

In a 1993 *UNESCO Courier* article, Carreras articulated his feelings about his art. "Above all," he explained, "it is the only channel through which I can express some of my deeper emotions. Although I'm someone who tends to keep himself to himself, when I sing I discover private feelings within me which I try to communicate to the audience. Singing is all about communicating. That's why

technique is important. The better your technique, the more likely you are to be able to communicate. But that's not enough. A singer must also be able, through technique, to inject life and substance into music, to give it a soul."

And where does music originate in Carreras' body and soul, and what route does it take before it resonates within his listeners? As he told Charlie Rose in 1994, a "song" begins in his heart, goes to his brain, and only then comes through the diaphragm to his throat. The brain, he said, is a kind of filter. But the music must start in the heart.

Below: José Carreras appears regularly not only in opera but in solo recital, a very different type of performance. Here, the singer must assume total responsibility for keeping the quality of the singing high, and for holding the interest of the audience—without the diversion of scenery, orchestral support, or the interaction with other singers.

The Rivalries

THE WILDLY PASSIONATE AUDIENCES THAT OPERA ATTRACTS CAN MAKE IT SEEM, MORE THAN ANY OTHER ART FORM, LIKE A COMPETITIVE SPORT. IF TWO POPULAR SINGERS (MOST OFTEN SOPRANOS OR TENORS) ARE NOT PERSONAL RIVALS, THEIR FANS WILL MAKE SURE THAT THEY EVENTUALLY WILL BE. SUCH COMPETITIVENESS MAKES COLLABORATIVE PERFORMANCES BETWEEN PERCEIVED RIVALS, LIKE THE THREE TENORS CONCERTS, ALL THE MORE REMARKABLE.

*Above: Domingo, Carreras, and Pavarotti acknowledge a capacity crowd of some
fifty thousand people during a concert in Vienna, 1996.
Previous page: The Three Tenors—Plácido Domingo, José Carreras, and
Luciano Pavarotti—have become so well-known as an entity, that no one ever asks,
"Which three tenors?"*

Although The Three Tenors are often seen as competitors, especially by the general public, there are substantial differences between them in the most basic characteristics of their voices—Domingo's and Carreras' have a darker quality and Pavarotti's a lighter one—and in their stage demeanor. Anyone who can walk onto the great opera house stages of the world and perform must, by nature, be somewhat outgoing, but there are vast differences in the ways in which performers present themselves.

It's interesting that Domingo and Pavarotti have been placed in competing positions as the top two tenors, because they are so very different. That they are both tenors is where the similarities end. Of the two voices, Pavarotti's is the lighter and has been able to reach into the outer regions of the tenor range more easily; Domingo's more "covered" Spanish sound is darker and, although he is able to get to the high C, he is not quite as at home there as is Pavarotti. (But he is, of course, able to reach down into

Above: The Three Tenors during a sound check at BC Place Stadium in Vancouver, Canada, in preparation for their 1996 New Year's Eve concert there.

Left: Pavarotti is, at once, the embodiment of the larger-than-life opera star and the approachable, loveable personality to whom his audiences can readily relate.

the top of his original baritone register for lower notes than Pavarotti can manage.) In demeanor, Domingo is reserved and quietly dignified, where Pavarotti is ebullient and extroverted. And Domingo has been spoken of as the more "serious" artist, whose interpretations are said to have more depth than Pavarotti's.

Pavarotti is the ultimate extrovert, making a connection with the audience the minute he emerges from the wings. He generates a positive energy that can power steamships, and he seems to get much of it back from his audience. Domingo is less the showman. But he is generally considered to be the better actor, more able than Pavarotti to involve himself in the personality of the character he is portraying. In his book *The Virtuosi*, Harold C. Schonberg stated, "When Domingo walked on stage, he demanded respect. When Pavarotti walked on stage, he demanded, and received, love and adoration." José Carreras, not completely in the same league of comparison and rivalry with his two colleagues, is more like Domingo than Pavarotti in his dignified but warm stage demeanor, although he is somewhat more gentle and not as strong or powerful a personality as his distinguished countryman.

In fact, the rivalry between The Three Tenors is really more between The Two Tenors than among the Three. For quite some time, Pavarotti and Domingo have been alone on the highest plane of tenor stardom, with an ongoing debate among their fans as to who should be called "the greatest tenor in the world." Carreras has been on the level just below.

Over the years, statements by both Pavarotti and Domingo have fluctuated between perpetuating the rivalry and saying that it did not exist.

Pavarotti seems to have the media eating out of his hand. Everything he does makes news; his dieting has been reported on the music, entertainment, news, food, and health pages. He has been photographed spouting

Right: Plácido Domingo's great strength and dignity are characteristics that define him, yet all that he does is imbued with warmth and a lack of egocentricity.

water in a pool like a human fountain, on horseback at the Columbus Day parade, singing with Frank Sinatra at Radio City Music Hall, and as the star of his own specials on nationwide television. Since the 1970s, Pavarotti has not been just a classical music figure; he has been a celebrity of the highest order and, because of his fame, assumed by the general public to be the greatest tenor in the world.

In a world that seems to confuse fame with greatness, one can understand any resentment that might have been generated on the part of Domingo. In a New York *Daily News* article by Stephen Rubin in 1980, titled "The Great Tenor War," Domingo is quoted as saying, "Anything Luciano does gets attention....So I have decided to join the fight...." Domingo felt that Pavarotti's representatives were trying to sabotage him, remarking that, "His [Pavarotti's] people even came out with the statement that I was not born in Spain but in Illinois, and that I was not born in 1941 but in 1935, the year of his birth. And they are serious. I cannot take it anymore. What is the matter with them? Is it fair," he continued, "that at *my* performances at the Met, I have to look at *his* face in the program and read, 'Pavarotti, the greatest tenor in the world, singing the greatest role of all, *Pagliacci*,' a role he has never even sung live? No. The moment of reality has arrived...."

Domingo discussed some of their basic differences in the same article: "When Pavarotti opened his mouth to sing, he was a tenor," Domingo says. "There was no doubt; here was a fantastic, beautiful and thrilling tenor, with complete tessitura, including some of the extras, like high C, D flat and D natural. I am a tenor who has worked for every half step. I haven't had easy high notes. Mind you, I think I'm improving, maturing and finding them easier, but if the public will just be excited by high notes, I will have a handicap....Italian voices have a more metallic quality; the Spanish voice is more velvety."

*Above: Pavarotti smiles at Carreras during the July 1994 **Three Tenors** concert at Dodger Stadium in Los Angeles.*

Pavarotti got his own shots in at Domingo in *TV Guide* in 1982, when he discussed bad taste, in relation to a television special Domingo had done in tribute to Enrico Caruso. "If anything is in bad taste, it's capitalizing on the famous names of others. On a recent NBC show, the tenor Plácido Domingo came out to 'celebrate' Caruso. Caruso, at this point in history, does not need celebrating."

But by 1983, the hard edge of competition seemed to be softening. In an autobiography published that year, Domingo had kind words for Pavarotti, saying that the rivalry had been more in the minds of others than in reality. And by 1993, in a *Time* magazine story titled "Two Knights at the Opera," Domingo denied that there were bad feelings between him and Pavarotti. "We are friends—and rivals."

Pavarotti later returned the kind feelings in *The New York Times* on February 14, 1978. "Did you see the *Otello* on television? Plácido made an *incredible* performance! So involved, in such vocal form, both together. The feeling he had for the entire performance was *incredible*, even for him...."

Carreras, on the *Charlie Rose Show* in 1994, was very open concerning his feelings about his colleagues, stating that, even though they were three very different artists, he admired certain aspects of both Pavarotti's and Domingo's artistry, particularly Domingo's, that he would not mind sharing. Concerning Pavarotti, he spoke of "the tremendous facility of this projection of the voice...and the power, of course, of communication...so easy and so perfect." And of Domingo, "I would like to have some of the aspects

Domingo has, like this incredible musicality, this incredible talent for music, besides the fantastic instrument. He is a fantastic actor, as well."

He downplayed the issue of rivalry among the three singers: "There is not rivalry between us. There is a kind of stimulating competition that brings us to try to do better." There was, he said, "...a lot of admiration, mutual support, and solidarity, and affection [in the Three Tenors concerts], and I think that came across in a very sponta-neous way." Even before the 1990 concert, Carreras had spoken of their mutual admiration and cooperation.

On the same program, Plácido Domingo had spoken about the support that all three singers had given each

other in the Rome concert. "We were really breathing—when Luciano was singing, José and me, we were breathing with him and vice versa....We were really encouraging each other."

Knowing what eventually happened, it is amusing to note Pavarotti's response in a 1982 New York *Daily News* interview, when he was asked about the possibility of his appearing jointly with Plácido Domingo. "Why?" he retorted. "I can do a concert by myself. There would never be a reason to do one with him." But with the survival and recovery of José Carreras, and the passage of time, one had evidently emerged.

Above: Despite the rivalries, there is a deep respect and genuine admiration for each others' work among the three singers.

The Concerts

THERE ARE RARE MOMENTS IN A PERFORMER'S CAREER WHEN SOMETHING VERY SPECIAL HAPPENS: A PERFORMANCE DEVELOPS A LIFE OF ITS OWN, TAKES FLIGHT, AND HAS AN INTENSITY THAT IS ALL-CONSUMING FOR THE PLAYER, ALL-INVOLVING FOR THE AUDIENCE. EVERYTHING CLICKS. EVERYTHING WORKS. THE MUSICIAN, OR ACTOR, OR DANCER BECOMES LOST IN THE WORK, UNAWARE OF THE PASSAGE OF TIME.

Above: The Tenors in rehearsal for their sold-out performance in Rome, July 1990.
Previous page: The theatricality of the Three Tenors concerts has thrilled many,
but has caused others to question the artistic value of the performances.
The favorable public response to the concerts resulted in unprecedented sales
of tickets, and of CD and video recordings.

It is a total involvement that focuses solely on the work, completely bypassing the ego. The legendary actress Helen Hayes, in her long career, said it happened to her only once, in a small-town theater. She was at a total loss to explain why it occured at that time, in that place. She was not aware of any special conditions in the theater or in her own life to explain it. It is an unforgettable experience for both performer and audience.

It is a pity that such moments are unpredictable even with the greatest artists, for, in this age of electronics, they could be recorded for posterity. One wonders how many have been witnessed only by small audiences and, considering the opposite situation, how many video and audio recordings have been released of routine performances that deserve to be quickly forgotten and not repeatedly experienced.

But the cameras *were* rolling in July 1990, at the Baths of Caracalla in Rome, when an unforgettable performance occurred for three singers who, ironically, had been professional rivals for years. The three artists' obvious pleasure in being together generated high spirits and an intense energy that were, to a great many, irresistible.

Above: The finale of the **Three Tenors** *concert in Rome, 1990: the last note of "Nessun dorma," the solo aria that was scored as a trio for the concert at the Baths of Caracalla.*

That a concert involving three competing artists happened at all is remarkable; for there to have been such good feelings among them was a bit of a miracle. But there were good reasons why it all happened.

At the press conference before the concert, Pavarotti said that the three singers had been approached a minimum of fifty times about appearing together. To be convincing to all three tenors, the idea apparently had to come from one of them, and it is José Carreras who is credited with bringing them together. Both Pavarotti and Domingo wanted to celebrate Carreras' return to good health and to opera. Without this reason to convene, the event probably would not have taken place at all; certainly, it would not have been as joyous as it was. In addition, all three singers are passionate soccer fans who would have found it difficult to resist a connection to the Italia '90 World Cup international soccer championship (which would be held right before the concert).

When the event was announced, it took only three minutes for all six thousand seats to sell out, even at prices reaching as high as $360 a seat. According to newspapers, one hundred thousand tickets could have been sold.

Every facet of the concert was planned to be spectacular. The emotional stage had been set with the Carreras

Above: The Three Tenors and conductor Zubin Mehta, at the press conference for the Rome concert, 1990.

celebration and the world-class sports event. The Baths of Caracalla in Rome (the open-air ancient ruins of a monumental public bathing house built between A.D. 212 and 216) provided a perfect historical backdrop. This magnificent example of ancient Roman architecture was dramatically lighted for the concert.

Nature, assuming the role of stage designer, provided a clear night and a full moon (which seems to hang in the sky like a prop in the concert video). Modern technology also took part, with all flights being routed away from the site—except for one plane that managed to get by, to which Carreras blew a kiss, just before singing "Il lamento di Federico" from Cilea's *L'Arlesiana*.

Zubin Mehta conducted an orchestra made up of more than two hundred musicians (double the size of a normal symphony orchestra) from both the Rome Opera and Maggio Musicale Fiorentino.

The concert began with the singers taking turns as soloists, first Carreras, then Domingo, then Pavarotti, until each had sung four selections. The last of these solos was Pavarotti singing "Nessun dorma," from Puccini's *Turandot*, which the BBC had chosen as the theme song for its coverage of the World Cup soccer matches. The aria had developed a life of its own for weeks before the games and the concert, and the audience roared with enthusiasm.

The first hint of the unusually spirited performances that would follow were the singers' exchanges of "high fives" as they passed each other mid-stage. They all hugged or touched each other in warm and supportive gestures as they passed on their way to and from the stage. Their excitement and delight were obvious.

The repertory was cleverly chosen by the singers to show themselves off to best advantage, and to please the widest possible audience. The gorgeous melodies, if not already familiar, could appeal to the uninitiated on first hearing.

When people speak about the magic of *The Three Tenors*, they are really speaking about the second half of the program, where the three singers performed together in the event's finale—a medley arranged by Lalo Schifrin of familiar and beloved works.

The opening songs in the medley were "Maria" and "Tonight" from Leonard Bernstein's *West Side Story*.

Below: Zubin Mehta, born in Bombay in 1936, has been music director of the Montreal Symphony, Los Angeles Philharmonic, and New York Philharmonic orchestras. He has held the same position with the Israel Philharmonic since 1968.

Above: *Domingo rehearses at the Baths of Caracalla, Rome, 1990.*

Despite the three singers' experience with popular songs, none seemed completely at ease. Each kept referring to the music, carefully negotiating his way through English after having sung in languages that were far more natural to them. With the classic Italian standard "'O paese d' 'o sole" and the Spanish "Cielito lindo," they were back in their element. Then came "Memory" from *Cats*, and they were plunged back into English, but now seemed a bit more comfortable.

The fun really began with a slightly hammed-up version of "Otchi tchorniye." "Caminito," lovely in its romantic sweetness, was little more than a bridge to the beloved, sentimental bouquet, "La Vie en rose," followed by "Mattinata." Before the applause could firmly take hold after each selection, Mehta would launch the orchestra into the opening bars of the next. In "Wien, Wien, nur du allein," Rudolf Sleczynski's salute to Vienna, the three took solo turns and sang in unison, then went on to a triumphant performance of the Spanish classic "Amapola." The intensity of the evening reached its peak with "O sole mio," first in a "straight," rather intense performance, then, after much onstage congratulating of each other and an onstage discussion, a fun-filled encore performance in which Pavarotti exaggerated his trills, which were parodied by Domingo and Carreras while Pavarotti looked on in delighted amazement. With his trademark handkerchief, Pavarotti wiped Carreras' moistened brow, and all three accepted a standing ovation from the Caracalla crowd. Mehta then signaled the orchestra and the strains of "Nessun dorma" rose again from the orchestra—dramatic and thrilling at the aria's last word, "Vincerò" ("I shall win!") and its obvious connection to José Carreras' fight for survival. The audience, witnesses to a rare event, rose again to their feet, with some people singing along.

At no point was there a hint of competition or ego on the part of any of the singers. All three were obviously secure and comfortable, with nothing to prove. They seemed to be having the time of their lives, and everyone was welcomed to their party.

Conductor Zubin Mehta, very much in the shadow of his three vocal colleagues, deserves more credit than he has been given. From the beginning, his involvement was total, with a degree of podium showmanship that, while perhaps not suitable in a concert hall or opera house, worked well in this setting. Although he was not completely responsible for the singers being "on," he could have seriously dampened the spirit had he not matched their mood and energy. This was an event in the truest sense of the word, and Mehta's influence added substantially to its excitement and intensity. But then, how could any conductor not react well to having more than two hundred excellent musicians follow every sweep of his baton?

The audience was drawn into the program by the quality of the singing and the irresistible appeal of having three superstar musicians sharing the same stage. The unusually relaxed, fun-filled atmosphere made the event seem like a big celebration and the musicians human and accessible.

Most important, however, was the contagious quality of their joy in making music, and in doing it together. They genuinely seemed to care about each other; Domingo and Pavarotti openly doted on Carreras.

For those who showed up after the three minutes in which the tickets went on sale, and sold out, the concert could be seen live on television in several countries. Reports vary as to the size of the broadcast audience. Even *The New York Times* blinked in disbelief at the huge size of the numbers. The day after the concert it reported that 800,000 had tuned in; the next day's edition corrected the number to 800 million! For classical music, which has always appealed to a relatively small percentage of the public, these numbers are massive. The viewers of this single program could have filled Carnegie Hall more than 266,664 times.

London/Decca Records knew what it had as soon as the concert ended. The company rushed the CDs into

Below: Domingo and Carreras share their thoughts while Pavarotti belts out a solo.

stores by mid-September, and the public rushed to buy them. To date, more than eleven million recordings and more than one million videos have been sold.

For people accustomed to the sales figures of popular music records, those for *The Three Tenors* may not seem impressive. But a classical music release will, on average, sell about 2,500 units within a year, depending on the popularity of the artist and the marketing support. The U.S. sales become even more impressive when one realizes that they did not have the tremendous promotional boost from the soccer games, which heightened European sales.

Numbers like this would not have been possible if sales had been limited to classical music lovers—even if every member of every family with an interest in classical music had purchased one. The phenomenal numbers involved "nontraditional" classical music consumers. People who had never before purchased a classical music recording were buying this one. Nothing like this had ever happened before. In the January 12, 1991, issue of *Billboard*, Lynne Hoffman-Engle, vice president of London/Decca Records, discussed the recording's "astonishing classical-to-popular crossover appeal." All types of people were

Below: **The Three Tenors** *1990 broadcast became the highest-grossing fund-raising program in PBS history.*

responding to the recording, which was "... being seen as a collector's item by many people of diverse backgrounds, ages, and musical tastes, from opera lovers to fans of rock." For a brief moment, Madonna was edged out of her number-one position by *The Three Tenors*.

The Three Tenors was the first classical music album to go gold; it has since gone platinum (selling more than a million copies) eleven times over. *The Three Tenors* laser disk became the first laser disk video ever to go platinum. In Europe, the recording of the aria "Nessun dorma" was selling like a pop single (due in part to the popularity of soccer); a Pavarotti recording of "Nessun dorma" went to the top of the British pop music charts, unheard of in modern classical music history.

The staggeringly high sales of the recordings did not depend solely on viewers seeing *The Three Tenors* broadcast, then running to their local record stores. The high sales were the result of a carefully orchestrated advertising campaign that exploited not only the traditional classical outlets but ones geared to the general public as well. Part of the strategy involved supplying edited recordings to pop radio stations and selling recordings in nonclassical music outlets such as K-Mart and Caldor department stores. Ads ran on trains and buses. Sales also benefited from media praise that bordered on hysteria. On ABC News' *Primetime Live* (July 1994), a reporter referred to The Three Tenors as "what someone called 'God's Trio,'" and as "...perhaps the greatest collection of classical talent ever assembled on one stage."

The success of *The Three Tenors* broadcast spilled over to benefit more than just the singers and their record company. The program became the highest-grossing fund-raising program in PBS history; New York City's Channel 13 alone raised more than $1 million from viewings of the tape. Repeated broadcasts of the program were seen on more than 125 stations, mainly during fund-raising periods.

But the stars themselves did not fare as well financially as they might have. Unable to predict the historic success of the recordings, the three singers had decided not to gamble on royalties, taking instead a flat fee of $500,000 each. The royalties would, of course, have resulted in figures many times their fee.

Within just a few weeks, "The Three Tenors" had become a household phrase around the world.

Above: **Joined by Conductor Zubin Mehta and orchestras from the Rome Opera and the Florence May Festival, The Three Tenors gave a truly memorable performance to their international audience.**

The Reunions

THIS IS THE AGE OF THE SEQUEL.

IT IS DIFFICULT TO THINK OF A SUCCESSFUL MOVIE OR MUSICAL EVENT IN THE PAST DECADE OR TWO THAT HAS NOT HAD A REPRISE. FOR *THE THREE TENORS*, IT TOOK FOUR YEARS TO HAPPEN. THE REUNION WAS DESIGNED TO BE ANOTHER SPECTACULAR EVENT, WITH A HUGE LIVE AND BROADCAST AUDIENCE, BUT THE 1990 CONCERT PROVED A HARD ACT TO FOLLOW.

Above: (from left) Domingo, Carreras, Pavarotti, and Mehta, Dodger Stadium, Los Angeles, 1994.

Previous page: Despite the rivalries assumed to be ever present between the most prominent singers in the opera world, Domingo, Carreras and Pavarotti share a deep appreciation of each other's work. Without this strong unifying basis, their collaboration could not have been successful.

Tibor Rudas, the Hungarian producer who had presented Pavarotti's huge stadium concerts for more than a decade, and who had produced the 1990 Rome concert, arranged another for July 16, 1994. This time, the concert was an official part of the World Cup soccer finals (the 1990 concert coincided with the finals but was not officially connected to them). The concert took place at Dodger Stadium in Los Angeles, before some fifty-six thousand people, with another 1.3 billion people in 120 countries tuned in electronically.

The concert producers said that the event cost between $12 million and $15 million to produce. In addition to artists' fees, there was the cost of designing and building a special stage in a section of Dodger Stadium known as "The Pavilion." This metamorphosis from ball park to concert hall required a week of labor by some six hundred workers. As Edward Rothstein reported in the *New York Times* four days after the concert, there were two four-story waterfalls pouring six hundred gallons of water per minute (before and after, but not during, the performance); a 440-foot-long backdrop covered by 2,500 cans of paint, creating a "rainforest paradise"; twenty fake classical pillars imported from Hungary; and thirty truckloads of greenery. A sophisticated sound system had speakers placed throughout the stadium, not just at the front of the stage.

Above: (from left) José Carreras, Plácido Domingo, and Luciano Pavarotti at the April 1994 press conference in New York announcing the first reunion of The Three Tenors, to take place in Dodger Stadium.

Above: Domingo and Carreras confer with producer Tibor Rudas during the Dodger Stadium concert rehearsal. Rudas was the mastermind behind the Three Tenors stadium concerts.

The program was, like the 1990 concert, a mix of operatic arias, traditional songs, and pop numbers, and included some selections repeated from the 1990 concert. This time, Zubin Mehta was limited to conducting just a normal-sized symphony orchestra, even though it was the 101-piece Los Angeles Philharmonic (with the sixty-voice Los Angeles Music Center Opera Chorus).

Rudas was quoted in *The New York Times* as saying that the ticket income for the new show was a "record take" for a musical event: $13.5 million for fifty-six thousand tickets priced from $15 to $1,000. If this is true, then there was little or no profit from ticket sales. But broadcast rights as well as CD, video, and laser disk sales would certainly compensate for that, as well as the considerable take from The Three Tenors merchandise, from clothing to sandwiches.

On ABC News' *Primetime Live* on July 14, 1994, Nancy Collins quoted Rudas as saying that the second concert took two years, and 274 pages of legal contracts, to arrange. This time, none of the principals repeated the

mistake made in 1990. Now the singers would get what they could: $1 million each, doubling their fees from the 1990 concert, and adding royalties from video and CD sales.

The record companies fought it out in a bidding war won by Warner Music Group, which guaranteed $10 million for CD, home video, and laser disk releases. Never before had so much money been invested in a classical music project. London/Decca, which had released the 1990 recordings, and which had a longstanding exclusive agreement with Pavarotti, agreed to release him for the 1994 recording only after it had won the contract for an audio-only version of "extra" material from the concert that Warner would not be using. Without London/Decca's consent, it would not have been possible for Pavarotti to appear on a new recording on any other company's label.

Again, "product" was rushed into stores—in less than two months, on the Atlantic Records label in the U.S., and on Teldec Classics, via Warner International, throughout the rest of the world. And again, the tenor-loving public scooped them up. More than eight million CDs, video cassettes, and laser disks of what was now called *The 3 Tenors in Concert 1994* were sold. Again, the strong sales were the result of both word-of-mouth communication and a very heavily orchestrated advertising campaign.

As part of the marketing strategy, The Three Tenors had filmed an invitation-only run-through concert in Monte Carlo one month before the Los Angeles concert; the "Brindisi" section (the well-known drinking song) from Verdi's *La Traviata* was used in promotional broadcasts that generated public interest in the Dodger Stadium recording, keeping the interest going from the time of the concert until the recordings were in the stores. An additional four minutes of video footage that showed the tenors at play in Monte Carlo was also made available to television outlets. Repeated broadcasts of the concert video on PBS also did not hurt sales of the recording in all three formats. The concert was a commercial success. But it was not an artistic one.

Despite the incredible ticket and recording sales, the sequel lacked much of what had made the first event so appealing. In place of the authenticity of the Caracalla Baths was a manufactured stage setting reminiscent of early Hollywood musicals, and unlike the first concert, the singers projected an almost forced camaraderie and enthusiasm.

In 1990, the music press had been either begrudgingly complimentary or downright critical. Peter G. Davis, in *New York* magazine, reviewed the performances from the recording (admitting, though, that they might have been more exciting in the flesh): "A stiffly managed medley of pop songs winds up the program, along with a bizarre three-way assault on 'Nessun dorma.' Listening to these well-known voices trade off phrases in a well-known Puccini aria [that was originally written for one tenor] has a certain horrible fascination—so does encountering an alligator in the bathtub. The curious may wish to try this one out once, before deciding on an appropriate method of waste disposal."

Below: The stakes were high for The Three Tenors' first reunion, in Dodger Stadium, 1994. Audiences and critics alike felt that much of the magic of the first concert was missing, that the concert lacked the exuberance and spontaneity of the 1990 concert in Rome.

Below: There was a lot to work out at rehearsals: four very different people had to agree on the interpretations of a wide variety of repertory. In addition to their stylistic and philosophical approaches, the singers and conductor had to work out the enormous technicalities involved in a long and complex program.

Eric Salzman's review in *Stereo Review*'s December 1990 issue was typical. He did not evaluate the concert in the context of a great artistic event, but got in the spirit of it. After discussing the strengths and weaknesses of each of the tenors, he put it all into perspective: "But let's not pontificate too much. This is not a festival performance of *Parsifal* but the great tenor-to-do of the twentieth century, and a great tumble of tenors it is, too. In short—if the expression can be pardoned under the circumstances—it's a hoot!"

Reactions to the reunion, from the press as well as the public, were almost unanimously negative. *People Weekly* wrote: "Four years after their smash 1990 Rome concert, Carreras, Domingo and Pavarotti finally reconvened in

July in Los Angeles's Dodger Stadium and the full—garish—Hollywood treatment. [The concert]...seemed underrehearsed, musically sloppy and downright patronizing to listeners...."

Time magazine, on December 26, 1994, was even harsher: "The Three Tenors II...the first time as an enchanting evening of song, the second time as an example of extreme bad taste and lazy greed. What was wonderful in Rome in 1990 was awful in L.A. as Luciano Pavarotti, Plácido Domingo and José Carreras sight-read their way through arias and show tunes on a set that included a waterfall. And no, the 'Brindisi' from *La Traviata*—the sequel's intended 'Nessun dorma'—did not fly to the top of the charts."

Many music journalists were outraged. The *American Record Guide* published a review of the CD in its January/February 1995, issue, writing: "...To dispose of one question at the outset: there is no musical value whatsoever in the concert....Nor do they take the music seriously...." It did not limit the blame to this day and age but to human nature: "...The great singers of yesteryear were every bit as ready to cater to popular tastes as those of today—Caruso and Gigli with Neapolitan street songs, McCormack with Irish ballads, Björling with Swedish folk songs, Tauber with Viennese schmaltz. Both Caruso and McCormack sang before crowds of up to 125,000 in outdoor amphitheaters, all of them appeared in bad movies, and Caruso even sang over the telephone to 3,000 San Francisco fans. There is not the slightest doubt in my mind that all of these singers would have been delighted to participate in events like the Los Angeles extravaganza."

The issue, however, is not that the singers of the past *performed* popular music, but *how* they performed it. Barrymore L. Scherer, author of the book *Bravo! A Guide to Opera for the Perplexed*, points out that the repertory of "canti popolari," Irish ballads, and Viennese waltz songs performed by singers like Caruso, McCormack, and Tauber, was, first of all, closer in idiom to standard classical music than modern pop songs are. Second, given the greater formality of their era, those singers performed this music more seriously than The Three Tenors did in their concerts. They did not toy or clown around with a song like "O sole mio," but approached it as they would approach an art song. Admittedly, in having their crossover fun, The Three Tenors were merely following a tradition going back at least to the 1950s in putting a contemporary twist on older popular repertory in an attempt to keep it fresh for successive generations.

To many musicians, that The Three Tenors used their voices for this kind of music was a travesty, like playing popular music on a Stradivarius. All three staunchly defend their pop-music involvement, saying that they received letters by the thousands from people who have become opera lovers because of them.

Domingo has repeatedly said that he has a natural proclivity toward pop music that stems from his zarzuela days. And he feels that singing pop music has had a beneficial effect on his operatic voice: "Since I started working lighter music back into my life, my singing in opera has, I think, become fresher and more intense. People usually go to the opera just to hear a beautiful melody, but in pop they want to hear the words, too, so you have to get very involved with the text. This is helping me to become even more conscious of words in an opera, to project character and verbal nuances more meaningfully—in my case, one kind of music is helping another."

Above: A giant screen was used to project the images of the performers to fans in all sections of the stadium.

*Above: In addition to singing in the
Three Tenors concerts, Carreras, Domingo,
and Pavarotti also participated in promotional events that would boost ticket sales
and sell CDs and videos of their concerts.*

children: "I remember that my daughters were not very interested in classical music until they heard a pop arrangement of a Mozart symphony. Then they said, 'Oh, Papa, this is incredible music!' So I said, 'The original is even more beautiful,' and I got it for them and they loved it. I don't care what vehicle brings them to it—if pop music or television is the way, then use it. And I will help this in any way—making beautiful performances on stage if it is possible, giving master classes, even doing American Express commercials or cooking spaghetti on a television show. The way we go to people doesn't matter much. We have to go to them." He also noted in the same interview, "The only big risk I have—and I know this—is that I am not taken seriously by some people because of these things...."

Following the commercial success of the Los Angeles concert, the tenors took their act on the road, embarking on their world tour, officially billed as:

MATTHIAS HOFFMANN PRESENTS
CARRERAS DOMINGO PAVAROTTI
WITH LEVINE
THE 3 TENORS IN CONCERT 1996/97
ANOTHER TIBOR RUDAS PRODUCTION

With conductor James Levine replacing Zubin Mehta, it included performances in Tokyo's Kasumingaoka National Stadium, on June 29, 1996; London's Wembley Stadium on July 6; Vienna's Prater Stadium on July 13; New York's Giants Stadium on July 20 (with seventy-seven thousand people present); Gothenburg, Sweden's Ullevi Stadium on July 26; Munich's Olympic Stadium on August 3; Dusseldorf's Rheinstadion on August 24; Vancouver, British Columbia's BC Place Stadium on December 31; Toronto, Canada's Skydome on January 4, 1997; Melbourne, Australia's Cricketground on March 1; Miami's Pro Player Stadium on March 8; and Barcelona's Stadium of the FC Barcelona. *Variety* reported on April 15, 1996, that the Three Tenors tour could gross more than $100 million.

The 1996 Giants Stadium concert, which received more press coverage than the other tour dates, probably because of its proximity to New York City, did not fare any better critically than the 1994 Los Angeles event. By now, many members of the public were echoing the music

Domingo strongly denies that by singing pop music he has sold out for the sake of the mass audience and the big paycheck. He feels that there is also a crossover effect that brings pop music lovers into the opera house. And into the record stores. In *New York* magazine on March 1, 1982, Domingo said, "If you could only see the hundreds of letters I have received here, in England, and in Spain for 'Perhaps Love.' 'We had never heard of Plácido Domingo before,' people write me, 'but now that we've listened to the record we have gone to see you in *Tosca* and *Hoffmann*—we have discovered the world of opera and we love it.'"

It is possible, however, that they have discovered Domingo, but not necessarily the larger world of opera. Doubt lingers about whether there is a substantial crossover effect, where people who have been introduced to opera by The Three Tenors will migrate from the stadium to the opera house, or if they will purchase recordings and videos by other artists.

Pavarotti, in the January 1980 *New York Times* article, "Pavarotti: As Passionate About Teaching As Singing," by Rosanne Klass, spoke of this happening with his own critics' opinions that The Three Tenors were investing very little effort in these concerts—in effect, taking the money and running. The cynicism of some critics seemed to betray a thinly masked anger toward the singers, not only for taking advantage of their audience members but for using the art form for their own advantage.

New York Times music critic Bernard Holland wrote a review on July 22, 1996, entitled "Popcorn, Traffic and, Yes, Three Tenors": "...With mouthfuls of popcorn, listeners chatted cheerily through the music and interrupted favorites like 'Nessun dorma,' 'La Donne è mobile' and 'Moon River' with cries of appreciation....Amplification precluded any strenuous attempts at subtlety....These men stand to clear $10 million each for a five-concert series. Perhaps a more apt title for these events would be 'Three Tenors, One Conductor and Four Accountants.' A brief intermission allowed Mr. Levine [conductor James Levine] plenty of time to fill out a deposit slip for the reported $500,000 he received for Saturday's event....For people who have lived their lives in classical music, *The Three Tenors* is a kind of benign tumor: unsightly but not life-threatening."

The tenors' representatives have said that there will not be future Three Tenors concerts. But a cause surfaced that might change their minds. La Fenice, the beloved historic Venetian opera house in which so many of the genre's greatest works, including many by Verdi, had premiered, burned to the ground in 1996. The singers openly discussed their desire to give a concert in Pavarotti's hometown of Modena to benefit La Fenice's reconstruction fund. With the ghost of Verdi looking over their shoulders, The Three Tenors will have a powerful source of inspiration with which to give their artistic best.

Despite all the negative criticism, tickets to the Tenors' concerts still sell by the thousands and recordings by the millions, and The Three Tenors remain a significant force in the music world. But there is one fact that cannot be argued: because it was conceived as a celebration of Carreras' life-and-death struggle with leukemia, the 1990 concert became a triumph of its own, a generosity of spirit where nothing was held back, where the importance of communicating with the audience became greater than the singers' individual egos. Whether or not the concert technically measured up to experts' criteria, whether or not it commercialized the arts, it has given a great many people a great deal of pleasure.

Below: The Tenors perform in **The Three Tenors Live in Tokyo** *concert at the National Stadium in Tokyo to start off their world tour on June 29, 1996.*

The Controversy…
and the Good News

IT IS NOT UNUSUAL FOR PROFESSIONAL MUSICIANS AND CRITICS TO LOATHE SOMETHING THAT THE GENERAL PUBLIC LOVES. *THE THREE TENORS* IS A PERFECT EXAMPLE OF THIS. NEVER BEFORE HAS A CLASSICAL MUSIC "PRODUCT" APPEALED TO SO MANY PEOPLE NOT PREVIOUSLY ATTRACTED TO THE ART FORM. AND YET THE RESPONSE FROM THE PROFESSIONAL MUSICAL COMMUNITY HAS BEEN ALMOST COMPLETELY NEGATIVE.

Above: Three singers in concert, in the truest sense of the word: coming together, in agreement.
Previous page: Throughout the past two centuries, opera has found a devoted audience, which now seems to be growing. Subtitles and surtitles provide simultaneous translations into the language of the audience, encouraging newcomers to venture into this traditionally exclusive world.

Many musicians and critics would like to have the word "classical" omitted from any discussion of *The Three Tenors*. In their opinion, the concerts are purely entertainment and not art, and should therefore not be taken seriously. *The Three Tenors*, to most musicians, is simply the dumbing down of classical music.

Why does this gap exist? What is it that music professionals hear that others do not? To gain insight into the attitudes of classical music professionals toward *The Three Tenors*, one must examine what the art is really all about.

Part of the wonder of classical music is its ability to satisfy people on many different levels, from the most basic enjoyment of a melody to the more sophisticated knowledge of the piece's form and construction, the relationship of word to tone, and the blend and balance of instruments and voices. Enjoyment can come from the awareness of strong emotion expressed through great restraint, of subtle changes of expression through the coloration of the voice or instrument, and from the delivery of a perfectly arched phrase and a beautifully realized

Above: Los Angeles concert, July 16, 1994.

111

Above: Token white handkerchief in hand, Pavarotti acknowledges an ovation during a concert at Avery Fisher Hall in Lincoln Center, which Zubin Mehta conducted.

characterization. It is about communication through pure sound, lush and beautiful when those qualities should be communicated, or harsh and ugly when those characteristics should be expressed. Truly great works and great performances do not tell all, but leave the listener to ponder the intentions of both the creator (the composer) and the interpreter (the performer), all processed and refracted through the listener's own psychology, philosophy, and life experience.

In bringing classical music to life, a performer's first priority should be to realize faithfully the intentions of the composer, whose system of notation communicates enough to provide the performer with solid guidelines about correct notes, relative loudness and softness, tempo, and other basic but critical elements of the piece. But the key word here is "relative"; the system of notation also provides just enough ambiguity to give the interpreter ample room to express his or her feelings through the music. There are, however, limitations to this freedom, imposed by what the composer has written as well as by the interpreter's knowledge of history and tradition. In every case, none of the decisions should be random; each must be made for a logical reason within the framework of the composition and its place in history.

To fully understand music one must be willing and able to look beneath the surface, to recognize the difference, say, between what a character states and what that character means. It is about the power of subtlety, and the hidden message. One must listen very closely, or much of the gold can slip by unnoticed.

All of this contributes to why musicians are critical of "stadium" concerts. The subtle changes in coloration of a voice or an instrument that can convey so much are lost in amplification, and so the meaning of the work cannot be fully realized. Nor can an atmosphere of intimacy or of intense involvement be established in a venue accommodating fifty or a hundred thousand people. For opera, a specially built hall (seating about three to four thousand people) is usually the largest in which detail and subtlety can be communicated. Built vertically, opera houses allow the audience to be within reasonable proximity of the singers, to hear unamplified voices, and to feel some intimate connection to the performers. Giants Stadium and Dodger Stadium provide a very different type of experience.

While none of these facts can be debated, what can be questioned is whether the subtler gesture matters at all to the great majority of listeners. Classical music, in its purer form, does not seem to appeal to the masses, and so one wonders if a classical musician must "sell out" by ignoring what the composer wanted, to appeal to the less refined sensibilities of the greatest number of people. Not all musicians, great or otherwise, are interested in appealing to the masses. Many are content with a career that includes appearances in the major opera houses and concert halls of the world and making good recordings, coming to terms with the fact that million-dollar fees are not worth what they would consider to be artistic compromise.

Such considerations are not limited to performances, but extend also to the marketing of classical music recordings and videos. There have been situations where a musical work has been performed with integrity, but the album cover or advertising materials have been designed in a prurient or attention-getting way. Aside from issues of bad taste (which are always highly subjective), there may be misrepresentation involved as purchasers can be disappointed with the nature of the product enclosed.

The Three Tenors came along just at a time when classical music began to confront a serious problem: diminishing and aging audiences that are not being replenished. Symphonic music (with its lack of visual appeal and its abstractness) seems worst off, with chamber music (and its relative intimacy) a bit more successful. In general, classical music is facing a critical problem: it is an art form that rarely appeals to a large segment of the public, and yet it may be dependent on doing just that to continue its existence. The art, particularly opera, is extremely costly to produce, with many participants involved in producing a "product" that, unless it is recorded (and the great percentage of performances are not), has no commercial afterlife. Ticket sales usually pay for only part of an opera company's (and an orchestra's) expenses, and so most performing organizations depend on subsidies—governmental, private, and corporate—to secure their existence. There are many people, particularly in government and politics, who feel that if classical music cannot stay alive on its own, perhaps it should not continue to live. If not enough people care about it to provide adequate support, is it really important to the life of the country? Into this worrisome cultural climate came The Three Tenors, appealing to billions, and generating a very healthy profit.

They also generated a great debate: by putting a theatrical spin on most of what they sing, are they doing harm to the art of music, or are they stimulating a beneficial interest in it? If audience members do not know that a performance is technically weak but derive genuine enjoyment from it, have they been done a disservice? These are, after all, people who did not choose between The Three Tenors and a performance at the Met; they probably would not be attending any other performers' concerts. They are interested in only The Three Tenors, or someone like David Helfgott.

Helfgott is another recent phenomenon in music, but he differs greatly from The Three Tenors as his success has little to do with music. The subject of the popular movie *Shine*, he is an emotionally disturbed pianist who at one time had great promise as a musician. People come to his concerts to see a personality, the survivor of an abusive childhood, who suffered for the cause of his art. They are delighted to see the underdog now triumphant, the tragic figure now victorious, finally playing on the great stages of the world—Avery Fisher Hall in New York's Lincoln Center, Boston's Symphony Hall, and elsewhere. And he is easy to champion: always joyful, always "up."

His illness has manifested itself in a manner that is quite appealing: childlike, Helfgott jumps up and down in excitement, impulsively (or compulsively), hugs and kisses everyone within reach, and sings and gestures eccentrically at the keyboard. With his story and his personality, he is an ideal media subject (who, by the way, might be appropriating precious media exposure that could be used to better advantage by a more "serious" artist, if indeed that artist would be given media space at all). But Helfgott could not attract audiences without the success of the movie behind him, and the publicity that has accompanied it. In spite of the fact that his playing is badly flawed on every level, his concerts sell out. And critics continue to shower him with devastating reviews.

Is music a casualty in this case? Perhaps. If Helfgott had been composing and performing his own works, there might be less of a problem. But he is performing masterpieces—his "signature" piece is the Rachmaninoff

Below: David Helfgott, the subject of the 1996 film, Shine, *in concert.*

Third Piano Concerto — and this work has not been properly presented by him. What he is playing is not what Rachmaninoff wrote. And even if the notes were played correctly, his interpretation is very far off base. The audience is not hearing the Rachmaninoff *Third* at its best. But again, the argument can be raised that many people listening to Helfgott would not attend another classical musician's concert, and since they have enjoyed the experience, no harm has been done. They are not coming to hear the Rachmaninoff; they are coming to hear David Helfgott.

One of the most serious aspects of these phenomena is the confusion in our society of fame with greatness. Classical music newcomers can fall into the trap of holding Helfgott (or The Three Tenors, or any other truly great musician on one of their off-nights) as the standard of excellence. This is true not just in music, but in other fields as well. Left unmoved by a second-rate performance by a famous artist, listeners will place the blame, unfairly and incorrectly, on themselves, questioning their own ability to judge quality. Still another concern is that "correct" performances of works might seem less interesting to inexperienced concert goers than more theatrical interpretations.

Because of this escalated star system, performing arts presenters (administrators who program series of local performing arts events) are seeing a trend where the public is becoming increasingly slow to purchase tickets to concerts by any but the most famous artists. These artists receive enormous fees, so not many presenters can afford more than few of them a season. They must, therefore, book a greater number of lesser-known artists (who, by the way, may be of very high quality). But the public does not know their names, and are reluctant to give them a try. It is a double-bind situation that finds attendance at many music series decreasing.

People within the music profession feel that The Three Tenors are transmitting a dangerous message to the next generation of singers: that the singers may take extreme liberties with the music, changing the message of the composer to suit their own needs, and that much of an artist's motivation can be financial, satisfied only by performances that will appeal to the largest numbers of people. The relative intimacy of the opera house, which provides performers with only a fraction of the income of the stadium, might be less attractive to singers of the next generation.

Most troubling of all to musicians is, that with the necessary marketing that mega-events require, the focus is mainly on the performers and rarely on the music. The works themselves become secondary, relegated to being only vehicles on which the performer's career will be carried. Most musicians feel it is the music that is important; the performer should be in service of it — not the other way around.

Above: Pavarotti with Sting and other rock musicians. The tenor maintains that his popular music performances have attracted new audiences to opera.

But not everyone in the music field feels that The Three Tenors are potentially dangerous to the art. Bernard Holland may have been on target in the review of The Three Tenors' 1996 Giants Stadium concert when he wrote, "For people who have lived their lives in classical music, *The Three Tenors* is a kind of benign tumor: unsightly but not life-threatening." He did not perceive their performances as being seriously dangerous to the art of classical music.

This debate can go on endlessly with no definite conclusion drawn. But Holland has his point. At present, everyone seems to have what they want: The Three Tenors, with their unique brand of vitality and joy in making music together, will endure; whether they do additional performances or not, they will continue to grace television broadcasts and live on in sound and video recordings. And connoisseurs can continue to experience the art in the ideal atmosphere and good acoustics of the opera house. At present, there is enough of a demand to keep both alive and well.

THE GOOD NEWS

The word is spreading: an evening at the opera is an event.

Of all the classical musical arts, the one that seems to be thriving most of all is opera. With its combination of sound and spectacle it is able, in this visually sophisticated era, to attract more new fans than any other type of classical music. The fact that it tells a story also makes it more accessible than other, more abstract, types of music. Because of this, it seems to have a reasonably secure future: opera is appealing not only to the forty-something-and-over crowd that traditionally populates opera houses, but to those young enough to be their children.

Newcomers find the opera house most welcoming. Surtitles and sub-titles provide simultaneous translations in the language of the audience, and preperformance lectures help to demystify this "exotic and irrational entertainment" (according to Dr. Johnson).

To match the new audience members, there is a whole new crop of singers filling the stages. Among them are sopranos Reneé Fleming, Angela Gheorghiu, Sylvia McNair, Aprile Millo, Amanda Roocroft, Cheryl Studer, and Ruth Ann Swenson; mezzo-sopranos Cecilia Bartoli, Sonia Ganassi, Jennifer Larmore, and Anne Sofie von Otter; baritones Dwayne Croft, Thomas Hampson, and Dmitri Hvorostovsky; bass baritone Bryn Terfel; and bass Samuel Ramey. There are even a number of tenors among them, including Roberto Alagna, John Aler, Francisco Araiza, Jerry Hadley, Ben Heppner, Richard Leech, and Neil Shicoff.

With opera's current state of good health, one hopes that The Three Tenors and other artists will inspire emerging young talent and help them to negotiate the maze that is the art and business of opera, for from these young artists will come The Three Tenors of the next millennium.

Below: The Paris Opéra. The great old opera houses seem to have new life breathed into them with the recent upsurge of interest in opera. The unprecedented popularity of The Three Tenors, with their voices and images heard and seen everywhere, has focused new attention on the art form. On the edge of the new millennium, the venerable world of opera is being perceived as a source of excitement and enjoyment by traditional opera-goers as well as members of the younger generation.

Bakers Bibliographical Dictionary of Musicians. Revised by Nicolas Slonimsky. 8th Edition. New York: Schirmer Books, 1992.

Breslin, Herbert H., editor. *The Tenors*. New York: Macmillan Publishing Co., 1974 (Pavarotti chapter by Stephen E. Rubin).

Carreras, José. *José Carerras Singing from the Soul: An Autobiography*. Seattle and Los Angeles: Y.C.P. Publications, Inc., 1991.

Domingo, Plácido. *My First Forty Years*. New York: Alfred A. Knopf, 1983.

Grout, Donald J. (with Hermine Weigel Williams). *A Short History of the Operas*. 3rd edition. New York: Columbia University Press, 1988.

Hines, Jerome. *Great Singers on Great Singing*. New York: Limelight Editions, 1982.

Kesting, Jurgen. *Luciano Pavarotti: The Myth of the Tenor*. Boston: Northeastern University Press, 1996.

Lewis, Marcia. *The Private Lives of the Three Tenors*. Secaucus, New Jersey: A Birch Lane Press Book, Published by Carol Publishing Group, 1996.

Mayer, Martin. *Grandissimo Pavarotti*. Garden City, New York: Doubleday, 1986.

McGovern, Dennis and Winer, Deborah Grace. *I Remember Too Much*. New York: William Morrow, 1990.

Pavarotti, Adua (with Wendy Dallas). *Pavarotti: Life with Luciano*. New York: Rizzoli, 1992.

Pavarotti, Luciano and Wright, William. *My World*. New York: Crown Publishers, 1995.

Pavarotti, Luciano (with William Wright). *Pavarotti My Own Story*. Garden City, New York: Doubleday, 1981.

Pleasants, Henry. *The Great Singers*. New York: Simon & Schuster, 1966 and 1981.

Sadie, Stanley, editor. *New Grove Dictionary of Music and Musicians*. London: Macmillan Publishing Ltd., 1980.

Schonberg, Harold C. *The Virtuosi*. New York: First Vintage Books, 1988 (originally published as *The Glorious Ones*. New York: Times Books, a division of Random House, Inc., 1985).

Snowman, Daniel. *The World of Plácido Domingo*. London: The Bodley Head Ltd., 1985 (also: McGraw Hill, 1985).

PHOTO CREDITS